WRITTEN BY : Fang Zhaoyuan

TRANSLATED BY : Zuo Quanwen and Translation Studio

Porcelain

Highlights of
Auctioned Chinese Antiques

CNS | Hunan Fine Arts Publishing House

图书在版编目（CIP）数据

瓷器：英文 / 剑矛，方昭远编著. — 长沙：湖南美术出版社，2012.3
（中国古董拍卖精华） ISBN 978-7-5356-5229-4

Ⅰ.①瓷.Ⅱ.①剑.②方.Ⅲ.①瓷器（考古）—拍卖—中国—图集
Ⅳ.①F724.59-64

中国版本图书馆CIP数据核字(2012)第043047号

PORCELAIN OF HIGHLIGHTS OF AUCTIONED CHINESE ANTIQUES

PUBLISHER: LI XIAOSHAN

SUPERVISOR: ZHANG XIAO, YAN HUA

AUTHOR: JIAN MAO, FANG ZHAO YUAN

TRANSLATOR: ZUO QUANWEN AND TRANSLATION STUDIO

EDITOR IN CHARGE: LIU HAIZHEN, LIU YINGZHENG

PROOF-READING: CHEN YINXIA

GRAPHIC DESIGN: XIAO RUIZI, HU SHANSHAN,
SHU XIAOWEN

PLATE-MAKING: SUN YAN, XIONG JIE

ENGLISH EVALUATION: XIAO FANG

PUBLISHING AND DISTRIBUTION HOUSE: HUNAN FINE ARTS
PUBLISHING HOUSE (NO.622, SECTION 1, EASTERN BELTWAY
2, CHANGSHA, HUNAN, CHINA)

DISTRIBUTOR: HUNAN XINHUA BOOKSTORE CO., LTD.

PRINTING HOUSE: SHENZHEN HUA XIN PRINTING CO., LTD.

SIZE: 787 × 1092 1/16

SHEETS: 10

VERSION: MAY 2012, FIRST EDITION;
          MAY 2012, FIRST PRINTING

ISBN: ISBN 978-7-5356-5229-4

PRICE: USD $19.90/ CNY ￥98.00

CONTENTS

IV. Pottery and Porcelain of the Song, Liao, Western Xia and Jin Dynasties

V. Pottery and Porcelain of the Yuan Dynasty

VI. Pottery and Porcelain of the Ming Dynasty

VII. Porcelain of the Qing Dynasty / 120

VIII. Pottery and Porcelain of the Republic of China

Guide to the Use of This Series

1. "Highlights of Auctioned Chinese Antiques" comprises five volumes, namely, "Bamboo, Wood, Ivory and Horn Carvings", "Porcelain", "Jadeware", "Bronzeware" and "Ancient Furniture". Each volume contains around 150 representative items put up for auction from 1995 to 2010 at auctions held by dozens of auction companies from cities like New York, Nagel, London, Hong Kong, Macau, Taipei, Beijing, Shanghai, Tianjin, Nanjing, Guangzhou, Kunming, Chengdu and Jinan. The selection of the items is based on the style, texture, form, decorative pattern, workmanship, function, cultural implication and value of the antiques in question, including some items which have not yet been transacted.

2. Each volume retains the original record of auctions and the items are arranged in order of dynasty, name, dimension, transaction price (or estimate price), auction company, date of transaction and item analysis.

3. Due to different origins of auction companies, the prices of the antiques in US dollar, Euro, Great Britain Pound, Hong Kong dollar or Taiwan dollar, have been converted into RMB according to current exchange rates.

Preface

A General Survey of Porcelain Auction

Jian Mao, Fang Zhaoyuan

The pottery and porcelain auction market of China has been brisk and prosperous over the past ten years due to both the social background in general and the features of pottery and porcelain in particular. With the rapid development of China's economy in recent years, people's income has been on the rise. The problem of subsistence, namely, food and clothing, has been solved, and there has been more and more surplus purchasing power, making it possible for people to buy "collected items", hence the saying "collecting things in times of prosperity". China is the home of porcelain. As a quintessence of China, porcelain, brittle but not easy to rot, has been a part of Chinese culture for several thousand years. Its exquisite plastic art and jade-like glaze are much appreciated, and decorative patterns, calligraphy and paintings on it make it even more elegant and beautiful. Unlike pure arts and crafts such as calligraphy and paintings, which are solely owned and appreciated by the "refined and sophisticated" few, porcelain is mostly daily utensil for the general public. Therefore, most people start collection with porcelain. According to a statistics, porcelain collectors constitute the overwhelming majority of the nearly 100 million artware collectors, resulting in a huge and brisk porcelain auction market. On the other hand, the market is flooded with forgeries and there are people who rack their brains to make imitations and fakes.

I. Keen collection injecting vigor into the auction market

There has been a dramatic increase in the number of porcelain collectors in the past ten years owing to the rapid economic development in the past decade. In some fast-developing cities, like Shanghai, Beijing, Guangzhou and Shenzhen, the per capita GDP in the year 2001 reached USD 3,000 or USD 4,000. In the following years, many provinces caught up, and in 2006, the per capita GDP in China's inland cities and countryside was USD 2,046. According to "Theory of Human Motivations" by Abraham Harold Maslow, man will begin to pursue higher spiritual needs after he has satisfied his needs of subsistence. Viewed from the law of development of international arts and crafts collection market, the collection market of a country or a region will get started when its per capita GDP reaches the critical point of USD 3,000 to USD 4,000. More and more Chinese have been involved in the collection, purchase and sale of artware or antiques, and the majority of them have become collectors of pottery and porcelain. Of all the collectors, there are different groups of people and their purposes vary. In terms of education, there are illiterates and Ph.D. supervisors. In terms of profession, there are farmers, workers, entrepreneurs, public servants, experts and scholars, and in terms of geographical distribution, there are people from inside China and people outside the country. Porcelain is a magic made of the rotten and is a "golden touch", a contribution of ancient China to the whole mankind. Pottery and porcelain are an important carrier of traditional Chinese culture, as they were with along the Chinese ancestors for the longest period of time and a wealth of them remains till today. From their first appearance in the Neolithic Period, pottery and porcelain were closely related to the daily life of the Chinese, widely used as tablewares, production implements, storing tools, building materials, ornaments, burial objects and so on. Up till now, they are still an important part of people's everyday life. Owing to different needs and aesthetic concepts of different time periods, there have been changes in the categories, designs and decorative techniques of pottery and porcelain in the course of inheritance. It can well be said that the history of pottery and porcelain is a history of the social life of ancient China.

Since the Tang Dynasty when Changsha Kiln first decorated porcelain with calligraphy and painting, the most characteristic of Chinese culture, porcelain gradually has integrated with calligraphy and painting arts, thus becoming refined and elegant and acquiring more artistic and cultural elements. The function of porcelain as an important carrier of Chinese culture explains why it is sold at extremely high prices at various auctions. Meanwhile, it is acid- and corrosion-proof and remains lustrous over thousands of years, therefore, it constitutes most of the articles and fragments unearthed from ancient tombs and historical sites, and there are now a large number of items handed down from generation to generation. In contrast, other ancient articles did not have this advantage. Firstly, they were not enough old. Antiques of bronzewares, ironwares, silk, lacquerwares, calligraphy and painting, and jadewares either appeared comparatively later in time or disappeared soon after their appearances, or never became popular in society. For example, calligraphy and painting arts were exclusively for the "meat-eating" nobles and intelligentsia, and jadewares were luxuries of nobles and the rich for daily life or ritual ceremonies, beyond the reach of the general public. Secondly, there were exacting requirements for the preservation of other antiques. For instance, silk, painted wooden utensils and paper calligraphy and paintings were all organic articles and were vulnerable to rot caused by mildews and insect bites. Buried underground for a long period of time, few of them could be well preserved. Easy to get rusty, bronzewares and ironwares were also hard to preserve. That is why they are so few now.

The workmanship of ancient pottery and porcelain of earlier time periods varies greatly from that of later time periods, and quality also differs dramatically even in the same time period due to different needs. This results in world-apart differences in their prices, which meets the needs of collectors with different economic strengths.

In a word, the emergence of large numbers of porcelain collectors with the increase of the economic strength of our citizens demonstrates that a considerable number of Chinese have shifted from the pursuit of practical materials to the pursuit of cultural taste, and the latter is a conscious behavior with which to absorb nutrition from traditional culture and should be encouraged and advocated, as this shows that our national quality is being raised. On the other hand, the ever-increasing number of people investing in antiques such as porcelain demonstrates that our fellow citizens have further extended their economic horizons. "Economy" has found its way into more and more fields, and this shows that the national economic consciousness and the economic control of our citizens are being enhanced.

II. Investment of capital in arts and crafts

With the boom of the collection market and the expansion of the profit margin of collection investment, the incentive of profit has begun to draw vast amounts of capital to the art market. The profit margin of stock market and real estate is getting narrower and narrower because of frequent slumps, great fluctuations and increased risks of the former and the strict control of the latter by the central government. However, compared with other kinds of investment, investment in artwares involves fewer risks with a return not necessarily worse than present-day stock market. According to an investigation, the mean return rate of investment in the financial sector is about 15%, that in the real estate sector is 20%, and that in artware collection is well over 30%. The high rate of return has attracted vast amounts of investment. According to a rough statistics, the art industry of China yields products worth about RMB 1,000,000 million, and the market value of artwares has far exceeded RMB 400,000 million. In 2010 alone, arts and crafts worth more than RMB 52,000 million were auctioned in China. As indicated in "Hurun Fortune Report of 2010", rich people in China mostly invest in real estate and manufacturing industries, and the sources of their fortune are mainly investment return and enterprise ownership. Optimistic about the prospect of China's economic development, this group of people favors investing in real estate and stocks, but at the same time they have begun to shift to the collection of watches, jewelry, ancient calligraphy and paintings, pottery and porcelain. At present, a "Wenzhou Army" has entered the collection market and many a coalmine owner in Shanxi has started to show a keen interest in artware investment. A report says that an investment of approximately RMB 100,000 million has flowed into China's artware market. With the expansion of the wealthy group of China, the ever-increasing purchasing power for arts and crafts will be the long-term support of China's artware market. Art collection has become the third hot spot of investment, right after stock investment and real estate investment. In addition to individual capital investment, some financial establishments, such as banks, start to invest in artware collection. The unique Chinese porcelain, like the panda of China, has become a "target of promotional hype", by which it will make its way to the market and to the world. This market fever has also attracted the attention of financial organizations. At present, financial establishments, including Merchants Bank of China, have started to take arts and crafts as their targets of investment and have come up with art products for investment.

Investment in fine porcelain involves relatively smaller risks. Some insiders indicate that many investors not only pay great attention to the exquisiteness and rarity of porcelain, but also determine its margin of appreciation in the investment principle of "Rare things are precious". This will both push up the prices of fine artwares and at the same time spur the whole artware market.

III. Publicity by the media

It is now a major feature of modern life to receive vast amounts of information released by the media. The media has no doubt acted as a catalyst from the time when people take an interest in antique collection to the time when they become collectors. It is the media that helps people realize the joy of collection and the potential of appreciation, and gives them relevant knowledge about collection and ways of appraisal. We can say that the media have cultivated and fostered such great contingents of collectors, including collectors of pottery and porcelain. Meanwhile, the media have profited a lot from the publicity and promotional hypes of arts and crafts.

The collection market has brought about TV programs on collection, which in turn has promoted the rapid development of the collection market and the growth of collection contingents, and has helped the general public know about collection, making "collection" a household name. The collection market and such TV programs have acted both as cause and effect. A mere reflection of the relationship between the media and the collection market in recent ten years reveals some very interesting phenomena. As early as 1999, Beijing TV and some local TV stations launched special programs on collection. By 2003, TV programs on collection mushroomed all over the country and the ratings were gradually on the rise. The most influential was the weekend program entitled "Appraisal of Treasures" of CCTV's Economic Channel on the basis of its "Artware Investment". All these programs were designed for the general public and very soon became the hot programs of the media concerned. The final of "The First Meeting of Treasure Competition" reached an unprecedented rating of 1.9%. According to a rough statistics, there are now more than ten TV stations in China which broadcast TV programs on collection every week. Weekly programs on collection are broadcast by over twenty TV stations across China , such as "Archives of National Treasures" of CCTV, "Horizon of Treasure Collection" of Zhejiang TV, "Collection Horizon" of Beijing TV, "Gateway to Henan, China" of Henan TV, "Treasures of the Land" and "Masters of Chinese Calligraphy and Paintings" of Shaanxi TV, "Collection in Times of Prosperity" of Shenzhen TV, "Treasure Collection in West China" of Chengdu TV, "Treasures in Times of Prosperity" and "Calligraphy and Painting Arts Weekly" of Changchun TV, "Archives of Rare Treasures" of Shanxi TV, "Record of Rare Treasures in Times of Prosperity" of Kunming TV, "Art ware Collection and Auction" of Tianjin TV, "Art Player" of Hunan TV, "Investment in Collection" of Phoenix TV, "Collection" of Shanghai TV and "Collections of My Home" and "Center of Fine Arts" of China Education TV. The ratings of these programs have been on the rise, fluctuating around 1%, thus becoming new profit increase points. Besides, there are now special digital TV channels broadcasting all over the country, such as "Horizon of Collection" of Shandong TV, and calligraphy and painting channels of digital TV specializing in calligraphy and painting arts and artware investment, such as the Calligraphy and Painting Channel of Central Digital TV. In addition to the TV media, the print media, including some influential newspapers, have set aside special columns on artware collection. In Shanghai alone, Xinmin Evening Newspaper has a number of special weekly columns on artware collection, such as "A Guide to Auction", "Private Collection" and "Determination and Appreciation of Rare Treasures", and other newspapers, like Jiefang Daily, Wenhui Daily, Morning News and Labor Daily, also carry special editions on artware collection. There are also such magazines as "Collection", "Collectors" and "Horizon of Cultural Relics". The annual average business turnover of advertisements on artware collection in newspapers and magazines in

China increased at the rate of 300% from 2001 to 2005. In order to raise the ratings of programs on collection, many TV stations have hired celebrities to be their hosts. Ma Weidu, a famous collector and connoisseur, is now the host of "Art Player" of Hunan TV; Wang Gang, a famous actor and collector, is the host of "Collection Horizon" of Beijing TV; Chen Duo, a well-known CCTV host, is the host of "Artware Collection and Auction" (originally hosted by Yang Yi, a cross talk actor); and Cao Qitai, a famous talk show host from Taiwan, is the host of "Investment and Collection" of Phoenix TV. All the programs are informative, interesting, fashionable and entertaining. Some programs have an eye-catching "Treasure Smashing" link for the purpose of "eliminating the false and retaining the true". At the same time, some programs adopt the approach of interactive quiz to determine treasures for the general public, and then tell the audience, through the experts, how to examine collected articles and determine their prices. Some media even organize province-wide or nation-wide treasure competitions to enhance the audiences'interests of participation and to attract them to the contingent of collectors.

When reporting on the auctions of Chinese arts and crafts at home and abroad, the media focus on the high prices of auctioned articles in order to evoke the frenetic desire of people for the profit of collection. The soaring prices of the Yuan Dynasty Blue-and-white Pot with Pattern of "Guigu Descending the Mountains", the Enamel Colored Bowl with Pattern of Spring Swallows in Apricot Forest dating back to the Reign of Emperor Qianlong of the Qing Dynasty and the Enamel Colored Revolving Vase with Pattern of Unbounded Auspiciousness dating back to the Reign of Emperor Qianlong of the Qing Dynasty have made people realize the huge profit of porcelain collection.

In spite of the different comments on programs and columns on collection, the media have undeniably made contributions to the cultivation of collecting contingents.

IV. The volume of transactions rocketing year by year

Calligraphy/painting and porcelain are two backbones of China's arts and crafts auction market. But 20 years ago, pottery and porcelain were regarded as "unpopular stocks", because the unit price was low, the transaction volume was much smaller than that of calligraphy and painting, and there were even times when large numbers of potteries and porcelain were transacted in package deals. However, pottery and porcelain have become quite a hit of collection and their transactions have been soaring up. First of all, let's take a look at the business volume of artware auctions in recent years. According to statistics, in 2002, there were fifty-nine corporations specializing in artware auction, with a total business volume of over RMB 2,000 million; in 2003, there were 171 artware auctions, with a total transaction volume of RMB 2,500 million; in 2004, there were 338 auctions, with a total transaction volume of RMB 5,700 million; in 2005, there were 604 auctions by 80 companies, with a total transaction volume of RMB 13,408 million, more than double that of 2004; in 2006, affected by the global financial crisis, the growth rate notably slowed down and there were 837 auctions, with a transaction volume of RMB 15,000 million; the transaction volume of 2007 was RMB 22,300 million; that of 2008 was RMB 19,194 million; in 2009, 141,165 of the 199,495 articles were auctioned, with a total transaction volume of RMB 21,250 million; and in 2010, the transaction volume of Chinese art ware auction reached RMB 57,300 million, constituting 33% of the global market share and ranking first in the world.

The rapid increase of the total business volume has indirectly reflected the increase of pottery and porcelain business volume, whose market share has been getting larger and larger. In 2003, porcelain was about the same with calligraphy and painting in market share: of the top 100 auctioned articles in terms of price, 53 were porcelain. But in 2003, the calligraphy and paining market was too brisk for porcelain to contend with. In 2004, nearly 30 auction companies in China held 60 ancient Chinese porcelain auctions, with a transaction volume of nearly RMB 1,000 million, making up 17.5% of the total, a record high for the first time in the history of the ancient Chinese porcelain auction. In 2005, 6 of the top 10 auctioned articles in terms of price were porcelain, each at the price of over RMB 20 million. In recent years, 36 of the top 100 auctioned articles in terms of price were ancient Chinese porcelain, which was a full evidence of the important position of pottery and porcelain in the artware market. The total transaction volume of Chinese artware auction market in the first half of 2007 was RMB 7,579 million, and that of porcelain sundries reached RMB 2,950 million, constituting 39% of the total of artwares. From the above figures, we can see that the "overlord" position of calligraphy and painting on the auction market has been taken by porcelain sundries. Compared with the autumn of 2009, the number, transaction and total transaction volume of porcelain sundries in the spring of 2010 further increased, with a total transaction volume of RMB 3,418 million. Porcelain auction market in the autumn of that year was extraordinarily brisk. As indicated in "Chinese Artware Market Survey for the Autumn of 2010" by AAMMC (Arton Art Market Monitoring Center), 15,789 items (26.62% of porcelain sundries) were on auction, with a total transaction volume of RMB 4,200 million, a 134% increase over the previous season.

Meanwhile, the number of special auctions of pottery and porcelain increased. From May 12, 2002 to March 17, 2007, 30 auctions were held, with a transaction volume of about RMB 196 million. In 2004, 60 ancient Chinese porcelain auctions were held by nearly 30 auction companies, with a transaction volume of nearly RMB 1,000 million and an average transaction rate of 67%, a record high for the first time in the history of ancient Chinese porcelain auction. A case in point is Hanhai Auction Company. In 2004, its total transaction volume of porcelain and sundries was RMB 86 million in the spring, and soared to RMB 240 million in the autumn. In 2005, it was RMB 130 million in the autumn, rose to RMB 180 million in the autumn and reached RMB 200 million in the spring of 2006. In 2007, Beijing Hanhai held 16 auctions, of which were as many as 8 for porcelain, jadewares and miscellaneous artwares. 131 of the 168 porcelain of different time periods were auctioned, with a transaction rate of 77.97% and a transaction volume of RMB 93.192 million. Besides, Sungari International added a porcelain auction in 2007 to its spring auctions; in 2008, Guangzhou Guardian held a special Shiwan Pottery auction; and there is the annual international pottery and porcelain expo in Jingdezhen, Jiangxi Province.

It was the same with Hong Kong auction market. From the transaction volume of HKD 143 million in 2001, the transaction volume of porcelain sundries of Hong Kong Sotheby's was on the rise. In 2004, Sotheby's held a special auction of "Chinese porcelain and art wares", at which 9 of the top 10 in terms of price were porcelain, one being the Vase with Famille Rose Twining Flower Pattern and Concave Brocade Design on Carmine Ground (dating back to the Reign of Qianlong of the Qing Dynasty) auctioned at the price of HKD 41.5024 million, creating a new world record of the auction price of Qing Dynasty porcelain of the year. In the same year, Hong Kong Christie's held a "Dragon and Phoenix Rare Treasures" auction with porcelain as the theme, at which the auction of the Blue-and-White Vase with Dragon and Phoenix Pattern (dating back to the Reign of Yongle of the Ming Dynasty) reached the climax and was auctioned at the price of HKD 26.38376 million, ranking third in the transaction prices of Chinese porcelain in 2004. The Celadon Vase with Double Dragon Handles (dating back to the Reign of Yongzheng of the Qing Dynasty) was auctioned at a record-high price in ancient Chinese single-color glaze porcelain. The total transaction volume of 2007 exceeded HKD 1,100 million. The focus of attention and prediction was the special auction of "Chinese Porcelain and Artwares" held by Hong Kong Sotheby's in the spring of 2009, because there was the "Eight Exquisite Treasures: Special Auction of Qing Palace Imperial Porcelain Collected by Europeans" in addition to the usual "Special Auction of Chinese Porcelain and Artwares".

Overseas porcelain market has followed suit. The total transaction volume of the special auction of "Chinese Porcelain and Artwares" of New York Sotheby's was USD 87.304 million. 228 of the 374 at the auction were transacted, with a transaction rate of 61%. Porcelain before the Yuan Dynasty demonstrated very good business prospect.

V. Surprisingly high unit prices appearing frequently

The changes of the international prices of pottery and porcelain are usually reported by "London Art News" after its annual evaluation of the pottery and porcelain market indexes, which are constructed on the basis of "collective evaluation". Each index consists of 20 articles, including pots, vases, incense burners, bowls, cups and plates, which were sold by London Christie's and Sotheby's in 1975. Each article in this group is evaluated twice by auction experts and its price is converted into US dollars at the monthly average conversion rate of the year in question. The year 1975 was decided upon because Sotheby's and Christie's, two leading auction companies of the world, began to auction Chinese porcelain in the 1970s. At present, the two companies are leaders dealing with the auction of Chinese porcelain and dominating the Chinese porcelain market. Many sky-high prices are created by these two companies. At an auction by British Railway Retirement Foundation in 1989, a Tang Dynasty Tri-color Glazed Horse was auctioned at the price of GBP 4.15 million (bought by the owner at the price of GBP 220,000 in 1978). At an auction of Hong Kong Sotheby's in May 1989, a Yuan Dynasty Blue-and-white Jar with Pattern of Opera Figures in a Courtyard was sold at the price of HKD 3.08 million (bought by British Railway Retirement Foundation at the mere price of GBP 143,000 in 1977). At the autumn auction of Hong Kong Sotheby's in 2005, the Imperial Enamel Colored Double-ear Vase with Pattern of the Moon Pavilion, Flowers, Rocks, Pheasants and Poem Inscription (dating back to the Reign of Emperor Qianlong of the Qing Dynasty) was auctioned at the price of HKD 122 million, a world record in Qing Dynasty porcelain auctions. This was more than 500 times that of the transaction price of GBP 16,000 30 years ago in London in 1975.

The following are more examples showing the sky-high prices of collected articles at various auctions.

In 1989, a Tang Dynasty Tri-color Glazed Horse was auctioned by Hong Kong Sotheby's at an unexpected price of HKD 49.55 million, and a Guan Kiln Brush Washer of the Southern Song Dynasty was auctioned by the same company at the price of HKD 22 million.

In 2002, a Famille Rose Olive-shaped Vase with Bat (happiness) and Peach (longevity) Pattern of the Reign of Emperor Yongzheng of the Qing Dynasty was sold by Hong Kong Sotheby's at the price of HKD 41.5 million.

In 2003, an Enamel Color Bowl with Flower and Rock PatternS of the Reign of Emperor Qianlong of the Qing Dynasty was auctioned by Hong Kong Sotheby's at the price of HKD 29.1824 million.

In 2004, the Vase with Famille Rose Twining Flower Pattern and Concave Brocade Design on Carmine Ground dating back to the Reign of Emperor Qianlong of the Qing Dynasty was sold by Hong Kong Sotheby's at the price of HKD 41.5034 million. The Celadon Vase with Double Dragon Handles of the Reign of Emperor Yongzheng was sold at the price of HKD 17.4237 million.

In 2005, the Blue-and-white Pot with Pattern of "Guigu Descending the Mountains" of the Yuan Dynasty was bought by a British collector at an auction of London Christie's at the price of HKD 230 million, and (the Imperial Enamel Colored Double-eared Vase with Pattern of the Moon Pavilion, Flowers, Rocks and Pheasants and Poem Inscription) of the Reign of Emperor Qianlong of the Qing Dynasty was sold at an auction of Hong Kong Sotheby's at the record price of HKD 122 million.

In 2006, the Imperial Enamel Colored Bowl with Pattern of Spring Swallows in Apricot Forest of the Reign of Emperor Qianlong was sold at an auction of Hong Kong Christie's at the price of HKD 151 million, and the Underglazed Red Vase with Twining Peony Pattern of the Reign of Emperor Hongwu of the Ming Dynasty was sold at an auction of the same company at the price of HKD 82.23 million.

In 2007, the Famille Rose Happiness and Longevity Bowl with Branch Pattern of the Reign of Emperor Yongzheng of the Qing Dynasty was sold at an auction of Hong Kong Christie's at the price of HKD 50.212 million, and the Blue-and-white Vase with Pattern of Dragon Playing with Pearls of the Reign of Emperor Yongle of the Ming Dynasty was sold at an auction of the same company at the price of more than HKD 49 million.

In 2008, the Jun Kiln Sky Blue Glazed Bell-shaped Flower Pot of the Ming Dynasty was sold at the price of HKD 39.527 million, and a Guan Kiln Green Glazed Vase of the Song Dynasty was sold at an auction of Hong Kong Sotheby's at the price of HKD 67.52 million.

In 2009, the Green Glazed Pieced Revolving Vase Set with Japanese Banana Leaf in Relief and Pattern of Twining Peony of the Reign of Emperor Qianlong of the Qing Dynasty was sold at the price of HKD 47.7 million, and the Famille Rose Pierced Revolving Vase with Pattern of Abundant Auspiciousness of the Reign of Emperor Qianlong of the Qing Dynasty was sold at the price of GBP 51.6 million in China.

The situation in Mainland China has also been brisk. In 1995, the Blue-and-white Flat Ribbon Gourd-shaped Vase of the Reign of Emperor Yongle of the Ming Dynasty was sold at an auction of Beijing Hanhai at the price of RMB 12.1 million. In 2006, the Famille Rose Medallion Vase with Pattern of the Eight Immortals Crossing the Sea of the Reign of Emperor Qianlong of the Qing Dynasty was auctioned at the price of RMB 52.8 million, and the Famille Rose Colored Gilded Pierced Incense Burner with Flower Pattern of the Reign of Emperor Yongzheng of the Qing Dynasty was sold at the price of RMB 26.432 million.

VI. Distinct categories

One of the most noticeable changes on the porcelain auction market in recent years is that each special porcelain auction has a particular theme. A category of articles is on auction at a time. Porcelain wares are divided either according to their categories, for example, incense burners, brush holders, etc, or according to their decorative techniques, such as blue-and-white, famille rose, enamel color, clashing color and single-color glaze; either according to their features of production, like imperial kilns or private kilns, or according to different time periods. This reflects that collectors have greatly enhanced their abilities and have begun to pay more attention to the cultural connotation of antiques.

1. Blue-and-white, and underglaze red porcelain: an eternal theme

The Ming and Qing Dynasties are the heyday of the history of Chinese pottery and porcelain. Jingdezhen was the symbol of the pottery and porcelain industry and the leader of technology of the two dynasties. The imperial kilns were the backbones of its pottery and porcelain industry and gathered the best craftsmen of the country of the time. New products, technology and styles were constantly developed in line with the requirements of the imperial courts at all cost, and quality was above everything else. All these account for the exquisite workmanship of products and the sky-high prices of collected items on current auction markets.

2. Colored porcelain: dazzling charm

As the name implies, colored porcelain refers to those applied with color(s), other than blue-and-white porcelain. These include underglaze color, overglaze color and clashing color which combines both overglaze color and underglaze color; overglaze colors are subdivided into red and green color, five-color, plain tri-color, famille rose color, enamel color and light purple color, and underglaze colors include underglaze red color, underglaze brown color, underglaze green color, underglaze tri-color and underglaze five-color. Such techniques reached their climax during the Ming and Qing Dynasties. A lot of collected items belong to these categories and are transacted at very high prices.

3. Single-color glaze: a huge potential

Single-color glaze porcelain refers to porcelain with only one color, which is both elegant and exquisite. Collectors tend to think that this kind of porcelain does not have the complicated techniques of colored porcelain or the cultural content of calligraphy and painting, and the auction price is always low. But we have to realize that it is quite difficult to make such porcelain due to its exquisite workmanship and exacting requirements. Flaws on such porcelain are more conspicuous than on colored porcelain and the number of existing items is very small. Imperial kilns in the Qing Dynasty paid much attention to the making of such porcelain and there were exquisite products of different styles and patterns, which are sold at high prices nowadays.

4. Blue-and-white porcelain of the Yuan Dynasty: an up-and-coming category

Blue-and-white porcelain originated in the Tang Dynasty, developed in the Yuan Dynasty, prospered in the Ming Dynasty and reached its peak in the Qing Dynasty. The Mongolians were strong, straightforward, bold and unrestrained, which was reflected in the porcelain of the time, making them distinct and unique in the aesthetic taste of the traditional Chinese nation. Much attention was paid to the raw materials, workmanship and styles of porcelain making, resulting in a number of fine items, which now draw the attention of collectors and are auctioned at high prices.

5. Porcelain of the Song Dynasty: a black horse

The Song Dynasty witnessed the prosperity of ancient Chinese porcelain. All the five famous kilns of the time, namely Ru Kiln, Jun Kiln, Ge Kiln, Guan Kiln and Ding Kiln, had distinctive features of their own and produced a large amount of porcelain exquisite in workmanship and unique in style. With the thriving of the pottery and porcelain market, porcelain of the Song Dynasty has become a black horse. There are a number of occasions on which such porcelain were sold at very high prices at a number of auctions.

6. Imperial Kiln porcelain towards the end of the Qing Dynasty: an income stock

The quality of porcelain produced in imperial kilns was closely connected with the rise and fall of the dynasties concerned, and this is true with the Qing Dynasty. Towards the end of the Qing Dynasty, the quality, design and innovativeness fell far behind earlier times. However, there were still a limited number of fine items in certain time periods and in certain categories. It is just the good quality of the small number that has attracted the attention of collectors and has led to the high prices at auctions.

7. Collections from overseas: late comers

Since 2005, more and more collected porcelain have been coming back to China and auction markets have become their transaction platforms. In 2005 alone, over 50,000 returned and constituted 40% of all auctioned artwares. In recent years, the number of returned porcelain and the volume of transaction have been on the rise. Due to the price differences at home and abroad, more and more auction companies vie with each other to get items from overseas and have them auctioned on the domestic market in order to acquire huge profits.

8. Export-oriented porcelain: a new member on the domestic market

Export-oriented porcelain refers to porcelain made to meet the demands of foreign market, which is different from those for the domestic market in design, style and decorative pattern. This may conflict with our traditional aesthetic concepts. It takes time for the Chinese to understand, adjust to and favor such porcelain. With the return of porcelain from overseas, coupled with the archeological findings on the Pottery and Porcelain Road on the Sea, more and more people have taken an interest in export-oriented porcelain. According to analyses of experts, the salvage of the two sunken ships and the ever-increasing attention of collectors to ancient Chinese pottery and porcelain have spurred the auction of pottery and porcelain.

9. Porcelain of the Republic of China: the spring time

Porcelain of the Republic of China refers to porcelain made from 1911 to 1949. The great craze for porcelain produced in imperial kilns of the Ming and Qing Dynasties and their rocketing prices kept the overwhelming majority of collectors at a distance. Collectors have to turn to porcelain of the Republic of China, resulting in a rise of price of 10 times in the past five years. During the Republic of China period, advanced porcelain-making equipment and technology were introduced and the quality of products was greatly enhanced. Porcelain of this time period was a product of both inheritance and innovation, thus representing an era and bringing about a number of fine items, which are now auctioned at high prices.

10. Modern porcelain: a promising category

Modern porcelain refers to porcelain produced after the foundation of new China in 1949. Due to the lack of historical accumulation, some collectors paid little attention to these items. However, as the market has been flooded with fakes and imitations, it is risky to collect ancient items. Many people have shifted their eyes to modern porcelain, which are new on the market. Modern porcelain, especially those made by famous craftsmen and artists, are a reflection of the high standard of porcelain making of new China. They are more artistic than ancient porcelain and are quite worthy of collection and investment. There are many examples of fine works and high auction prices.

VII. Recommendations for collectors

1. Be rational and genuine collectors

Genuine collectors collect pottery and porcelain out of interest, enjoyment and the appreciation of the artistic and cultural taste in their collections. They are pleasing to the eye and the mind, and can mould temperament. It is quite different from risky stock dealing, by which people expect to be rich overnight. It is true that collection can help preserve and add value, but making profits should not be the main or the only purpose.

2. Constantly enhance the ability of appraisal

The ability of appraisal can be enhanced by visiting various museums, appreciating relevant arts and crafts, consulting experts involved and reading related books in order to know more about pottery and porcelain. In this way, you will learn more about the workmanship and cultural content and be able to fully tap the inherent value of your collections.

3. Choose and decide what to collect according to your interest and financial means

It is practically impossible for one to have a thorough understanding and research of all potteries and porcelain due to their long histories, wide distributions and countless varieties. You may choose items from a particular kiln, a certain time period or a specific category, as this will be more effective and rewarding.

4. Seek new fields and items

Items in new fields are generally inexpensive and have not yet attracted people's attention for the time being. This is especially important for collectors with limited financial strength. In terms of time period, one may consider porcelain before the Yuan Dynasty, as, for various reasons, they are cheap in price, small in number and large in appreciation margin in the future. In terms of category, there are collectors who take pains to collect incense burners, lamps, tea sets, drinking vessels, etc. Ancient porcelain were so widely used that there must be some categories to which few people have paid attention. One can seek new items and new fields as he sees best.

I . Pottery and Porcelain before the Qin Dynasty

Painted Double-eared Pot

Origin: Yangshao Culture
Height: 42 cm   Width: 44.5 cm
Hammer Price: RMB 19,136
Name of Auction Company: Hong Kong Sino Art
Date of Transaction: 2006-07-29

　　This painted double-eared pot has a labial mouth, a short straight neck, a bulged belly and a flat bottom. As a piece of argillaceous red pottery, it has two circular ears in the middle of its belly and black colored grid patterns on its upper belly. Painted geometric design or animal-shaped pattern is the most distinct characteristic of Yangshao Culture, hence its another name Painted Pottery Culture. Pottery making workmanship was highly mature during Yangshao Culture Period, producing utensils and implements of regular and exquisite forms and styles. They were mostly fine clay red pottery and sand inclusion red pottery, and grey and black pottery was rarely found. The elegant painted decorative patterns are a reflection of the daily life and artistic creativity of the people of that time.

Colored Duck-shaped Pot

Origin: Yangshao Culture
Height: 23.5 cm
Appraisal: RMB 30,000
Name of Auction Company: Zhongpai International
Date of Transaction: 2006-05-20

This duck-shaped pot has a contracted neck, a slightly outward-sloping round mouth and an elongated gourd-shaped body, with an ear on each side, a fan-shaped tail and a small round foot. It is balanced, symmetric and unrestrained in style, with a plump form, exquisite workmanship and a smooth surface. Painted all over are broken lines and string patterns. With its fine and tough blank, it falls into the category of argillaceous hard pottery. It is now still in bright colors after thousands of years of vicissitudes.

Grey Pottery Jar with Painted Frog Pattern

Origin: Majiayao Culture
Height: 37 cm
Appraisal: RMB 28,000
Name of Auction Company: China Guardian
Date of Transaction: 2006-11-22

This grey pottery jar is a piece of argillaceous red pottery with a wide mouth, a thin lip, a short neck, a small flat bottom, a round bulged belly and a pair of ears. It is painted with bold black frog patterns, also called variant figurine pattern. The feet of the frogs are linked together. The lines of the drawing are fluent while changeable to coordinate with the model. Frog pattern was used as a common decorative design on painted pottery of the Majiayao Culture, which reflects the aspiration of ancient people for multiplication and breeding.

Black Pottery Pierced Long-handled Lantern

Origin: Longshan Culture

Height: 23.2 cm

Appraisal: RMB 6,000

Name of Auction Company: Pacific International

Date of Transaction: 2000-05-09

This lantern is made up of a plate, a long handle and a base. The plate is shallow and the handle is long with 13 symmetric pierced holes. It is painted black all over, without any lines or patterns. It represents the shape of lanterns in ancient China. The earliest lantern is derived from dou, a piece of pottery tableware used from the late Neolithic Period to the Warring States Period. Our ancestors placed wick and oil in the shallow bowl of dou to get light. Since then, this kind of lantern has been passed down for thousands of years, functioning as a light source for mankind.

Jar with Twining Rope Pattern

Origin: Warring States Period
Height: 29 cm
Hammer Price: RMB 283,360
Name of Auction Company: Hong Kong Chieftown
Date of Transaction: 2008-12-01

This jar has a big mouth, a short neck and a flat bottom. All over the body is woven design, which is covered with twining rope patterns. There is a sheep-head-shaped circular ear on each side of the shoulders. This jar is plump, and the twining rope pattern is orderly and unrestrained in style. The two sheep heads on the shoulders particularly add the finishing touch.

II. Pottery and Porcelain of the Western Han, Eastern Han, Wei, Jin and the Southern and Northern Dynasties

White Pottery Green Colored Female Figurine

Origin: Western Han Dynasty
Height: 102 cm
Appraisal: RMB 200,000
Name of Auction Company: China Guardian
Date of Transaction: 2006-11-22

This female figurine cups one hand in the other, with its hair divided from the middle, and a coil dangling to the shoulders. Its broad face was elaborately carved. It has plump cheeks, curved eyebrows, a pretty nose and a small closed red mouth. On the figurine, there are three straight-style long gowns, with crossed collars exposed ring upon ring. The innermost layer is red, the middle one is green, except for the edge, and the outermost one connects the long sleeves. This figurine consists of two models, for the head and the body were jointed together after being made separately. The hands were hidden in the sleeves and the feet in the flaring skirt. It is a method that saves many details while at the same time maintaining the fluency and integrity of the lines, and strengthens the stability of the whole figurine, clearly demonstrating China's ancient aesthetic concept. This is a relatively big figurine, made after the ancient customs of tall and slim stature. It shows a composed, respectful, cautious and solemn manner, a full embodiment of the style of the pottery figurine in the Western Han Dynasty and the exquisite technique of pottery in the Han Dynasty as well.

Primitive Celadon Double-handle Jar

Origin: Han Dynasty
Height: 33 cm
Appraisal: RMB 28,000
Name of Auction Company: China Guardian
Date of Transaction: 2006-11-22

This jar has an inward-sloping mouth, a flat rim, sloping shoulders, a bulged belly and a flat bottom. A pair of beast ears are decorated on the shoulders symmetrically. There are three double-stringed lines on the lug boss of the upper side of the jar. It is green glazed from the top to the belly, exposing a purple brown blank below. The green glaze on the surface is lustrous and moist, running downward naturally. Between the double-stringed lines, there are patterns of clouds and birds carved in a lively and graceful way. Phoenix pattern was one of the traditional patterns used on porcelain, first decorated on painted pottery during Neolithic times, and was used a lot afterwards. Phoenix was a divine bird from Oriental State Valuing Music and Rites from ancient legends. With a plump shape and fluent lines, this jar is a representative work of primitive celadon potteries of the Western Han Dynasty.

Green Glazed Pig and Sheep Pens

Origin: Han Dynasty
Length: 40 cm
Appraisal: RMB 35,000
Name of Auction Company: China Guardian
Date of Transaction: 2006-11-22

This is a piece of argillaceous grey pottery with pale green glaze. The whole article is in oblong shape and is made up of a sty and a sheepfold, each with a pig and two sheep. There is an awning on the fold and a toilet in each pen. This green glazed pen for pigs and sheep, made of low temperature glazed pottery, is a burial object. The unification of the shed and the toilet is a reflection of the habits and customs of people of the Han Dynasty.

Green Glazed Bear-foot-shaped Barn

Origin: Han Dynasty
Height: 28 cm
Appraisal: RMB 20,000
Name of Auction Company: China Guardian
Date of Transaction: 2006-11-22

This barn is a piece of argillaceous red pottery with pale green glaze. There are a ridge, ridge tiles and a round hole on the round top of the cylindrical barn and three bear-foot-shaped feet at the bottom. Three groups of string patterns divide the belly into four parts, and there are arc-shaped string patterns under each group of string pattern, though indistinctly. This barn is a burial object found as early as in the Warring States Period.

Green Glazed Human-shaped Lantern

Origin: Han Dynasty
Height: 26.5 cm
Hammer Price: RMB 3,080
Name of Auction Company: China Guardian
Date of Transaction: 2005-03-13

Lead was used as a very popular cosolvent in low temperature green glaze in the Han Dynasty. This green glazed pottery lantern is in the shape of a servant on her knees with a baby in her arms and a cylindrical lamp on the top of her head. The whole article is complete, massive, vivid in posture and concise in lines, which is a full demonstration of the artistic style of simplicity. This lantern is exactly like the one collected in Shanghai Museum, except for its lighter color of glaze.

Grey Pottery Pot with Colored Phoenix and Animal Patterns

Origin: Han Dynasty
Height: 42 cm
Appraisal: RMB 200,000
Name of Auction Company: China Guardian
Date of Transaction: 2006-11-22

This pot has a grey pottery blank with an open mouth, a contracted neck, a bulged belly and a round foot. A pair of red animal head applique rings are attached to the shoulders. The rim and the foot are both decorated with a circle of red brand splashed with white glaze. The patterns painted from the neck to the belly are a mix of white, orange, blue and brown colors, a motif known as phoenix design. The outline is sketched in white color, the other three colors are filled in it, and orange is also used to paint the five sense organs and feather texture of the phoenix. The phoenix spreads its wings and tail, and its postures vary from each other and the colors of its feather are plentiful and changeable. The painting style is flexible and graceful, making people feel comfortable. With a typical Han Dynasty style, this pot is well preserved and is rich in bright colors, making it a rare artwork of the Han Dynasty.

Colored Pottery Pig

Origin: Han Dynasty
Length: 26 cm
Hammer Price: RMB 327,750
Name of Auction Company: Chongyuan International
Date of Transaction: 2008-04-12

This plump and sturdy pottery pig falls into the category of argillaceous gray pottery. Its four limbs are short and strong and its tail is coiled on the buttocks. It is lifelike, and its look is charmingly naive, with its ears turning to the front and its snout and nose pointing to the front. The corners of the snout are up-warping, and the eyes are looking straight forward. On its feet are some red glazes, demonstrating that colored decoration was once adopted but has now pitifully peeled off.

Yue Kiln Celadon Heap-Molded Jar

Origin: Western Jin Dynasty
Height: 57 cm
Appraisal: RMB 250,000
Name of Auction Company:
Panlong Enterprise
Date of Transaction:
2005-12-16

The blank of this jar is dark grey, hard and heavy. The green glaze, even and vitric, now yellowing and cracking, does not cover the part near the bottom, which is earthly red. The lower half is a jar with four groups of the same hunting pattern, in which a rangifer tarandus rushes like a boar with a fawn running beside it and a gundog chasing behind, followed by a hunter with a bow and arrows slanting on his back. On the edge of the jar is a platform with an arch over the gateway in the front and at the back. On the left of the gateway kneels a courtling and on the right stands a man holding a flag. A watchtower is placed on each side and beside the left one is a stele in the shape of a turtle. Two groups of figurines stand on the third storey of the platform, each group with twelve figurines playing music. Those dancing, singing and side showing are in the first row, while those singing in harmony are at the back. In between are four players, one beating a drum, one playing the bamboo flute, one beating to the music and one playing the zither. The upper storey is a square platform, on which are four arches over the gateway and two pillars in the front. Four vats are placed at the four corners of the platform. On each vat, there are four legendary dragons and two birds. The dragons lie on the top of the eaves, above which is a loft with curved roofs and crested roosters standing on the peaks, eaves and ridges.

Yue Kiln Celadon Lion

Origin: Western Jin Dynasty
Length: 16 cm
Height: 12.5 cm
Appraisal: RMB 90,000
Name of Auction Company: Panlong Enterprise
Date of Transaction: 2005-12-16

This Yue Kiln celadon is in the shape of an imposing lion crouching on its feet. The lion has a strong body and glaring eyes. It raises its head, shows its teeth, and pricks up its ears, behind which is heavy mane. The lion has a beautiful beard under its jaw, wings and feathers are carved on the belly, and its tail is oblate. Caesious glaze, yellowing, thin, bright and cracking cover the whole ware except the bottom of the lion's feet.

Yue Kiln Brown Dotted Rooster Head Pot

Origin: Eastern Jin Dynasty
Height: 13.8 cm
Appraisal: RMB 110,000
Name of Auction Company: Panlong Enterprise
Date of Transaction: 2005-12-16

    This Yue Kiln brown dotted rooster head pot has a plate-shaped mouth, a contracted neck and a flat bulged belly. Its flat bottom is slightly sunken and on the upper belly is a rooster head spout. There are two loops in bridge shape on the shoulders symmetrically and a plate is connected to the mouth. This pot is fine and smooth with the color of its glaze even and clear, and cinerous color flashing with yellow. Near the bottom are irregular red spots. The pot is underglazed with brown spots to form a geometric pattern.

    This rooster head pot is famous for its rooster-head-shaped spout and it was popular from the Western Jin Dynasty to the early Tang Dynasty, until it was replaced by new types of handled pots in the early Tang Dynasty.

Deqing Kiln Black Glazed Rooster Head Pot

Origin: Eastern Jin Dynasty

Height: 39 cm

Hammer Price: RMB 127,200

Name of Auction Company: Zhenguan International

Date of Transaction: 2003-10-26

This pot has a plate-shaped mouth, a narrow neck, a round belly and a flat bottom. There is a rooster-head-shaped spout on one side of its shoulders, and a curve handle on the other side, slightly higher than the spout, linking up the shoulder with the mouth. There are a pair of loops in the shape of arched bridge between the spout and the handle. The whole pot is black glazed except for the part near the bottom which reveals the blank. The upper belly is carved with a circle of lotus petal pattern. The pot is of classic elegance, power and grandeur. Its glaze is glossy and shining black. This handle pot is surely a masterpiece among the Deqing wares of the Eastern Jin Dynasty, resembling the one collected in the Palace Museum in Beijing. In Chinese, "rooster" is pronounced the same as "auspicious", so the use of rooster head as a decoration on the pot means an auspicious and peaceful future.

Celadon Toad

Origin: Southern Dynasty

Length: 18 cm   Height: 18 cm   Appraisal: RMB 160,000

Name of Auction Company: Panlong Enterprise

Date of Transaction: 2005-12-16

A base with a lotus foundation rests atop this toad. The base is inlaid with a rectangular jin (an ancient Chinese character which means a bar for placing wine cups), on which are five urns. The toad's all fours are sturdy and strong, and its belly is lifted from the ground, ready to jump up at any time. It raises its superciliary ridge, with its round eyes bulged and the mouth grinning. The material of this ware is hard, and its green glaze, now yellowing, is thin and cracking. This article is novel, visual, lively and vigorous. With the elaborate workmanship, deep sense of antiquity and exquisite modeling, it is worth collecting and researching.

Hongzhou Kiln Celadon Bowls (one pair)

Origin: Southern Dynasty
Diameter: 15.6 cm
Appraisal: RMB 20,000
Name of Auction Company: Shenzhen City
Date of Transaction: 2006-06-18

This bowl has a restrained mouth, a deep arc belly, a round cake-shaped foot and a flat bottom with no glaze, and with a grey white blank. The bowl is painted with greenish yellow glaze which is lustrous and elegant. On the face of the glaze are some fine-iced crazes. Besides, the glaze is of a strong sense of glass texture and is plain, and smooth without grains. Hongzhou Kiln was one of the six most famous kilns in the Tang Dynasty. It got its name from its location in Hongzhou, which is present-day Nanchang in Jiangxi Province.

Grey Pottery Colored Male Figurine

Origin: Northern Wei Dynasty
Height: 41 cm
Appraisal: RMB 80,000
Name of Auction Company: China Guardian
Date of Transaction:
2006-11-22

This male figurine wears a small hat, a loose sleeve garment and tight drapes. With his hands folded before his chest, the man wears a mild expression and a broad smile. His garment and head are red glazed, and the rest is white glazed. The features of the figurine were very popular in the Northern Wei Dynasty, the form and the structure were gentle and beautiful, tall and straight, and their facial features were sweet. This pottery figurine reflects all these traits well, so it is regarded as a work of the Northern Wei Dynasty, resembling a painted figurine collected in Luoyang Museum in Henan Province.

White Glaze Green Colored Bowl

Origin: Northern Dynasty
Diameter: 11 cm
Hammer Price: RMB 9,350
Name of Auction Company: China Guardian
Date of Transaction: 2005-12-10

This bowl has a straight mouth, a deep belly, and a cake-shaped foot. Painted all over is faint yellowing white glaze with vertical bar-type green glaze on the belly. Regularly shaped, this bowl is decorated with vertical bar-type green glaze which is not very regularly arranged from the mouth to the belly, seeming to be of fantastic decorative effect intentionally or unintentionally. Judging from the form of the ware and the features of the body glaze, this bowl can be a product of north China. It represents the rough features in the initial stage of white glaze with green color.

III. Pottery and Porcelain of the Sui, Tang and Five Dynasties

Yue Kiln Lidded Pot

Origin: Sui Dynasty
Height: 18.2 cm
Hammer Price: RMB 1,240,500
Name of Auction Company: Hong Kong Sotheby's
Date of Transaction: 2005-03-31

This pot has a straight mouth and a slanting shoulder with six square loops. It slopes from the belly to the bottom, and the bottom is flat, yet a little concave. Its lid is round and takes the shape of a lotus. The body is painted with yellowing celadon glaze except for the bottom. In the central part swells a circle of overturned lotus petals which divide the body into two parts with the upper part ornamented with two layers of stamps.

Tri-color Glazed Double-dragon Vase

Origin: Tang Dynasty
Height: 36 cm
Appraisal: RMB 120,000
Name of Auction Company: China Guardian
Date of Transaction: 2006-11-22

With the rim folded outward, this vase has a thin neck with three dimpled bow string patterns, an elongated and round belly and a flat bottom. The mouth and the shoulders are connected with two dragon-shaped handles decorated with three pearls on each, each dragon holding the mouth of the vase in its mouth. It is painted with semi-glaze, with white, green and yellow piebald tri-color glaze on the upper part of the body and no glaze on the lower half. The whole article is elegant and exquisite.

Tri-color Glazed Candle Holder (one pair)

Origin: Tang Dynasty
Height: 27.9 cm
Hammer Price: RMB 843,540
Name of Auction Company:
Hong Kong Christie's
Date of Transaction: 2005-09-20

This candle holder is composed of a small plate and a large plate, connected by a cylinder with bow string patterns. There is a cup-like candlestick stand in the center of the upper plate. The round foot slopes outward and the whole body is painted with white, green and brown glaze, and the bottom is plain without any glaze. This candle holder has a regular shape, a primitive design, evenly-distributed glaze, bright and smooth quality and gorgeous colors. It is a first-class work of tri-color glazed potteries of the Tang Dynasty.

Tri-color Glazed Phoenix Head Kettle

Origin: Tang Dynasty
Height: 33 cm
Hammer Price: RMB 286,800
Name of Auction Company: Hong Kong Christie's
Date of Transaction: 2002-10-28

The spout of this kettle takes the shape of a phoenix head which holds a small pearl in its mouth. The kettle has a thin neck, an oblate belly and a flat bottom, with its high foot sloping outward. The whole body is painted with green, brown and white glaze with no glaze on the bottom. On one side of the kettle is a crank. On the belly are two sides of medallion pictures formed by plastic decoration, one side with a phoenix flying and the other side with a man riding on a horse and shooting. With the plastic paster decoration, the pictures on the kettle have the effect of basso-relievo, with distinguished images, smooth lines and flamboyant colors, and can be rated as an excellent artwork.

Wudai Horse with Twisted Clays

Origin: Tang Dynasty
Height: 27.7 cm   Appraisal: RMB 120,000
Name of Auction Company: Beijing Zhongjia
Date of Transaction: 2006-12-24

This horse stands upright with its ears pointing upward and its eyes wide open, showing its serenity. It is precisely shaped and well proportioned, and in particular, its straight and sturdy legs are very well presented. Horses were highly regarded in the Tang Dynasty for these reasons: the first was the Tang dynasty's blood relationship with the nomad; secondly, traveling on horseback was popular in this dynasty and both men and women preferred riding horses to sitting in the sedan; thirdly, polo was popular in the Tang Dynasty. Therefore, horses became an indispensable part of people's life. From existing archeological finds, we know that twisted clay crafts originated from the Tang Dynasty and flourished in the Song Dynasty. Beginning from the Yuan Dynasty and onwards, it gradually disappeared.

Yue Kiln Five-petal Plate with Dragon Pattern

Origin: Tang Dynasty

Diameter: 20 cm   Hammer Price: RMB 346,840

Name of Auction Company: Chongyuan International

Date of Transaction: 2006-10-05

This plate has an open mouth, a five-petal rim, a sloping belly and a round foot painted with glaze. There are fire marks of mud spots on the foot and the french gray blank is distinctive. The blank is fine and compact, with its glaze yellowing in blue. The surface of the glaze is bright, clean and shining with hacking in parts of it. Inside the plate are five groups of cloudlet decoration, each taking the shape of the Chinese character "pin" or the shape of three tadpoles. Besides, a circle of dint with a dragon grain is carved inside the bottom. The dragon raises its head and is flying upward with its mouth open, tongue wagging, palpus elegant and fluttering. The four feet are pedaling with three powerful and vigorous talons. The scales on the whole body are fine and well-proportioned. The dragon looks robust, powerful and imposing.

Lushan Kiln Brown Glazed Colored Kettle

Origin: Tang Dynasty
Height: 20.2 cm
Diameter of Foot: 9 cm
Appraisal: RMB 400,000
Name of Auction Company: Zhongpai International
Date of Transaction: 2006-05-20

    With the rim sloping outward, this kettle has a short spout, a flat bottom, a handle and two ears. It is plump, with its shoulders plump and round and its belly bulged. Its whole body is painted with brown glaze with four pieces of bluish white colored mottling. The two kinds of glaze fully blend with each other, making the kettle multicolored with an obvious appealing contrast. Therefore, this kettle is one of the exquisite artworks of fancy glaze porcelain from Lushan Kiln in Henan Province. Fancy glaze porcelain was called "fancy porcelain" in ancient documents, and it was a creation of the Tang Dynasty. Fancy glaze porcelain kilns are mainly distributed in Henan Province.

White Porcelain Buddhist Kettle

Origin: Tang Dynasty
Height: 17.5 cm
Hammer Price: RMB 77,000
Name of Auction Company: Shanghai Zhengde
Date of Transaction: 2006-06-30

This kettle has a straight and elongated neck, and a cake-shaped dharma-cakra. Its belly is round and bulged with a spittoon-shaped spout on one side of the upper part. The round foot slopes outward and the bottom is flat. Except for the bottom, the kettle is painted all over with white glaze which is bright and smooth, and yellowing in white. With the blank massy, compact and fine, this kettle is regularly shaped, simple but elegant. In addition, the whole surface of the kettle is plain and smooth, except for some ribs on the mouth. The Buddhist kettle, popular in Buddhist ceremonies and also known as Junchi, is made of pottery or metal to hold water. It is one of the 18 objects carried by Bhiksu, a Buddhist monk, and is used to drink water or wash things.

Glazed Colored Pot with Pattern of Female Figurine Playing Polo on Horseback (one pair)

Origin: Tang Dynasty
Height: 21.5 cm   Length: 21 cm
Hammer Price: RMB 3,671,720
Name of Auction Company: Chongyuan International
Date of Transaction: 2006-05-02

This horse is plump and sturdy, with its mane cut and tail bound, neck stretched and head raised. The horse is galloping with four hooves jumping into the air. A woman is bestriding the horse, with her body appressed to the saddle, and bending to the right. It seems that she is batting the ball. The horse is painted with yellow glaze, with its head and saddle plain without glaze, so does the woman. The plain blank is decorated with colored drawings, but unfortunately, some of this decoration has flaked away. This pottery figurines is lifelike and dynamic, showing a vivid picture of a horse which is whinnying and running about wildly and a woman who spares no effort on batting. These pottery figurine playing polo are in pairs, reflecting the rich imagination of craftsmen of the Tang Dynasty. The scene of women playing polo shows superb workmanship and exquisite craftsmanship.

Changsha Kiln Green Glazed Brown Colored Kettle with Poem Inscription

Origin: Tang Dynasty

Height: 17.2 cm

Hammer Price: RMB 79,200

Name of Auction Company: China Guardian

Date of Transaction: 2006-09-09

This kettle has an outward rim, a thick neck, a short spout and a handle fixed on its back. It has a melon-shaped belly and a flat bottom. The belly is inscribed with a brown glazed poem in running script which reads: "I will travel a thousand li since this departure; it is a long long time before we meet next time; there are 30 days in a month; I will miss you every day." This lovesick poem is not included in Complete Tang Poems, so it should have been a work of a folk poet, supplementing the poetries of the Tang Dynasty. Poetry is an important decoration for potteries of Changsha Kiln, and poems of the Tang Dynasty in various chirographies on pottery not only reveal the style and situation of calligraphy of the Tang Dynasty, but also illustrate the importance of poetry in the Tang Dynasty.

Changsha Kiln Green Glazed Brown Colored Kettle with Cloud Pattern

Origin: Tang Dynasty
Height: 20 cm
Hammer Price: RMB 98,325
Name of Auction Company: Chongyuan International
Date of Transaction: 2008-04-12

With the rim sloping outward, this kettle has an elongated neck, a plump shoulder, a bulged belly and a high round foot. On one side of the kettle is a long and thin curving spout; and on the other side is a curving handle. Lines on the kettle are smooth and varied. In this variation, the symmetry between the handle and the spout brings balance to the whole kettle. Besides, the adoption of a high foot makes the lines elegant, tall and straight. Painted all over is green glaze and on the surface are some tiny hackings.

Green Glazed Bulged Vase

Origin: Five Dynasties
Height: 21.5 cm
Hammer Price:
RMB 43,068
Name of Auction Company:
Hong Kong Christie's
Date of Transaction:
1999-11-02

This vase has an outward mouth, an elongated and contracted neck, a plump shoulder, a bulged belly, and a round foot sloping outward. It is painted with yellowing celadon glaze on which there are tiny hackings. With a regular and delicate shape, a fine blank and bright and smooth glaze, this vase is an excellent artwork from Yue Kiln.

Ⅳ. Pottery and Porcelain of the Song, Liao, Western Xia and Jin Dynasties

Ding Kiln Red Glazed Vase with String Pattern

Origin: Northern Song Dynasty
Height: 18.2 cm
Diameter of Mouth: 6.8 cm
Diameter of Foot: 6.7 cm
Appraisal: RMB 250,000
Name of Auction Company: Tianjin Emperor's Ferry
Date of Transaction: 2001-11-03

This vase has a trumpet-shaped mouth, an elongated neck, bended shoulders, a deep belly and a flat round foot. The blank is white and fine, painted with deep red brown glaze except for the bottom. With five string grains on the neck, lotus petals design on the shoulders and lotus facing upward, the decoration technique is adept and the lines are free and fluent. This vase is rarely seen in red glaze porcelain from Ding Kiln. There are many records of red glaze porcelain from Ding Kiln in documentaries and they were highly valued in the Song Dynasty.

Jingdezhen Green and White Glazed Pillow with Hornless Dragon Pattern

Origin: Northern Song Dynasty

Height: 15.5 cm

Length: 17.5 cm

Hammer Price: RMB 167,440

Name of Auction Company: Chongyuan International

Date of Transaction: 2006-05-02

The surface of this Jingdezhen green and white glazed pillow with hornless dragon pattern is like the shape of ruyi, engraved with twining lotuses. Two interlocking frolicking dragons support the pillow and are made by means of piling, different from traditional dragons. The dragons are powerful and balanced with vivid and exaggerated style, without the feelings of force and ferocity. On the contrary, it gives the feelings of naughtiness and loveliness. The shape of the base is oval. The pillow is painted with green and white glaze which is lenitive and transparent. The pillow is white, hard and thick, and the design is full of skills and imagination. The design is regular and varied.

Jun Kiln Sky-blue Glazed Sunflower-shaped Flower Pot with Saucer

Width: 22.2 cm
Transaction Price: RMB 4,218,800
Name of Auction Company: Hong Kong Christie's
Date of Transaction: 2002-05-07

This pot is shaped like a six-petal sunflower with a folded rim, a melon-shaped deep belly and a round foot. The inside and outside are glazed, with the rim iron black, and the outer wall is embellished with sky-blue glaze, and there is a tripod at the bottom. The bottom is carved with the Chinese character meaning "nine". Exquisitely and gracefully designed, and thoroughly and evenly blue glazed, it is a rare treasure produced in "Guan Jun (imperial Jun Kiln)".

"Guan Jun", called Numbered Chun Wares by Westerners, refers to porcelain wares such as wine vessels and flowers pots or vases, which are produced in the Jun Kiln and are printed or carved with numbers from one to ten in Chinese characters. Since most of them are treasures handed down from generation to generation, contemporary scholars classify them as "Hereditary Jun Porcelain" or "Ornamental Jun Porcelain" in order to differentiate them from such commonplace Jun porcelain wares as plates, bowls, stoves and pots unearthed from Jin and Yuan tombs and relics. Produced in imperial kilns for imperial use at the request of the imperial courts, they were called "Guan Jun (imperial Jun Kiln) porcelain wares, which are now mostly collected in Beijing Palace Museum, Teipei Palace Museum, Washington Freer Art Gallery and Harvard University Fogg Art Gallery, and a few are in official or private collections at home and abroad. There are at present disputes over the time periods of the production of these porcelain wares. Some people think that they were made in the Northern Song Dynasty, while others argue that they were produced during the reigns of Emperor Yongle and Emperor Xuande of the Ming Dynasty.

Yaozhou Kiln Green Glazed Sunflower-petal-shaped Plate Carved with Pattern of Duck Playing in Water

Origin: Northern Song Dynasty
Diameter: 18 cm
Hammer Price: RMB 98,440
Name of Auction Company: Hong Kong Christie's
Date of Transaction: 1998-11-03

This plate has an open mouth and a round foot. The inside wall, getting smaller towards the bottom, is carved with seawater patterns. In the center of the bottom, a swimming duck is carved. The outside wall is smooth with no pattern. The whole body is embellished in celadon, which is deep and green yellow. The bowl is shaped in a graceful way with a distinctive pattern. The duck pattern is vividly carved, reflecting the exquisite craftsmanship of Yaozhou Kiln. It is regarded as a representative work of Yaozhou Kiln.

Ru Kiln Lavender Grey Glazed Lid

Origin: Northern Song Dynasty

Height: 7 cm

Diameter of Mouth: 16.7 cm

Diameter of Foot: 12.8 cm

Hammer Price: RMB 35,200,000

Name of Auction Company: Beijing Zhongjia

Date of Transaction: 2008-10-26

This lid has an open mouth, an arched wall, a shallow belly, a flat base and a round foot. On the outer bottom there are the traces of five nails which were fired by bound foot. It is smooth and in pink and green color and has a natural network of cracking with neat modeling and exquisite workmanship. On the upper side is a lid and the whole body is in ash color. It is well preserved and considered as a fine product of Ru Kiln in the Song Dynasty.

Dengfeng Kiln Flask with Flower and Pearl Patterns

Origin: Northern Song Dynasty
Height: 41.2 cm
Appraisal: RMB 90,000
Name of Auction Company: Zhenguan International
Date of Transaction: 2003-10-26

This Dengfeng Kiln flask with patterns of flowers and pearls has a plate-shaped mouth, an elongated neck, a bulged belly and a round foot. On the shoulders encircle twining flowers. The top and the bottom are decorated with two string patterns. This vase is painted with the patterns of twining peonies and lotus petals underneath. There are also two string patterns on both sides of the patterns. The foot is bare without any glaze. The shape of the vase is stout, the patterns are bright and the lines are smooth, so it is regarded as a masterpiece of Dengfeng Kiln of the Northern Song Dynasty. There is a similar article in the Palace Museum of Beijing, but with a tiger pattern.

Yaozhou Kiln Green Glazed Plate Carved with Four Chinese Characters Meaning "Elegance" or "Gracefulness"(one pair)

Origin: Northern Song Dynasty

Diameter: 21.8 cm

Hammer Price: RMB 121,000

Name of Auction Company: Beijing Rongbao

Date of Transaction: 2007-06-10

This plate has an open mouth, an arched inner wall and a round foot. The inside and outside are embellished with green glaze and on the inside wall are four Chinese characters meaning "wind, flower, snow and night", which are decorated with curved grass. The blank of the foot is exposed. It is carved in a smooth and powerful way with a regular form, hard blank, smooth glaze, fluent carving and forceful inscription, making it a rare treasure of Yaozhou Kiln in the Northern Song Dynasty.

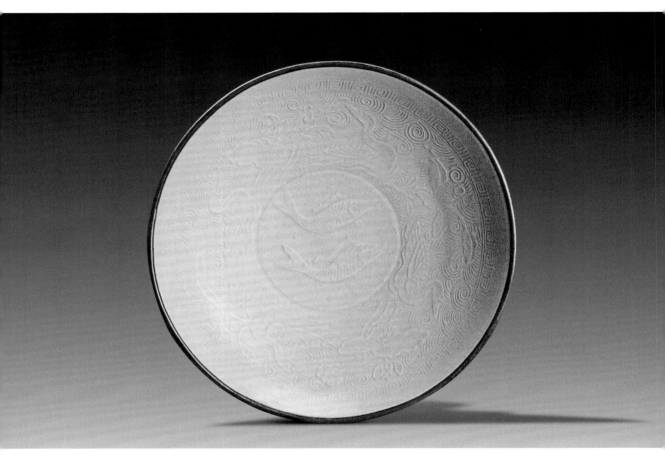

Ding Kiln White Glazed Plate with Pattern of Fish and Duck Playing in Water

Origin: Song Dynasty
Diameter: 16 cm
Hammer Price: RMB 307,625
Name of Auction Company: Hong Kong Christie's
Date of Transaction: 1998-11-03

This plate has an open mouth, a round foot and a shallow belly with brass buckles. The inside of the plate is decorated with patterns of fish and duck padding in the lotus pond; the center is ornamented with the design of a pair of fish. With all these realistic images, this plate is typical of the white glazed stamping wares from Ding Kiln. Ceramic whitewares were fired in Ding Kiln as early as the Tang Dynasty. Even though most famous porcelain at that time was Xing Kiln whiteware, the products from Ding Kiln can match with those from Xing Kiln. Until the Song Dynasty, Ding Kiln flourished while Xing Kiln declined. Hence, Ding Kiln whiteware became famous around the world instead of those from Xing Kiln, with the method of upside down firing. There is no glaze on the rim with a bare blank.

Caramel Flower Bowl

Origin: Song Dynasty
Height: 6.3 cm
Diameter of Mouth: 17.9 cm
Hammer Price:
RMB 748,000
Name of Auction Company:
Zhongpai International
Date of Transaction:
2006-05-20

This bowl has an open mouth, an arc belly and a round foot sloping slightly outward. The glaze is dark reddish brown, with a little reddish orange and iron black. And it is thin and evenly painted without hackings. The surface of the glaze feels as fine as jade and as lubricating as grease. Besides, the blank is thin and regular, and the clay is white and clean with clay bubbles. Inside of the bowl are three flowers stamped with curled petals and unfolded leaves. The bottom is decorated with a circle of string pattern with a stamped flower inside.

Yue Kiln Secret Glaze Bowl with Kid Pattern

Origin: Song Dynasty

Height: 5.5 cm

Diameter of Mouth: 16 cm

Hammer Price: RMB 2,860,000

Name of Auction Company: Zhongpai International

Date of Transaction: 2006-05-20

This Yue Kiln secret glaze bowl with kid pattern has an open mouth, a shallow arc belly and a wide round foot with the characteristics of bowls of Yue Kiln of the late Tang Dynasty and Five Dynasties. Both the outside and inside are engraved with two cupped string patterns with thin dents, mixed with auspicious cloud patterns. In the bowl is engraved with a boy with a halberd, hanging fish with auspicious ribbons, which are the symbols of good luck, auspice and sufficiency, and could usually be seen in the scene of praying for rain. It is the auspicious pattern loved by ancient people. The boy is naive and cute, and wears golden locks. He is wealthy and naughty with lively and lifelike expressions. There are marks of rectanglar supporting nails on the base. It is the characteristic of the secret glaze porcelain of Yue Kiln. The glaze is smooth in texture, and the green glaze is mixed with emerald which is the feature of the smoothly and evenly painted precious agate glaze.

Jizhou Kiln Black Glazed Bowl with Phoenix Pattern Dotted with Partridge

Origin: Song Dynasty

Height: 8.5 cm

Diameter of Mouth: 21.5 cm

Appraisal: RMB 120,000

Name of Auction Company: Zhongpai International

Date of Transaction: 2006-05-20

This black glazed bowl with phoenix pattern dotted with partridge has an open mouth, an inclined straight belly and a small round foot. At the bottom of the bowl stand cuspate bumps. It is the unique style during the process of pulling and repairing the blank. The center of the bottom is a circular nail-shaped bump. The body is grayish yellow, black glazed with brown, full of metal luster. There are hawksbill spots on the glaze. The exterior of the belly is decorated with free and fluent hawksbill spots. The interior of the bowl is decorated with waving phoenixes and leaves. The two phoenixes are flying through the branches. There are a ring of marks shaped like the Chinese character"回".

Longquan Kiln Five-tube Vase with Lotus Petal Pattern

Origin: Song Dynasty
Height: 14.6 cm
Hammer Price: RMB 495,000
Name of Auction Company: Beijing Seeks Antique International
Date of Transaction: 2006-03-19

This Longquan Kiln five-tube vase with lotus petal pattern has a plate-shaped mouth, a short and straight neck, inclining and sloping shoulders, a round foot and a round belly decorated with lotus petals. On the shoulders of the vase stand five straight and circular tubes with equal distance to each other. The tubes are hollow to the belly. The vase is painted with cyan-greenish glaze which is thick, lenitive, composed and mild, just like a first-rate beautiful jade. This vase is engraved with thin crackings. It is a typical pot of the Song Dynasty, which implies "a bumper grain harvest".

Cizhou Kiln Pillow with Tiger Pattern

Origin: Song Dynasty
Diameter: 32 cm
Hammer Price: RMB 164,625
Name of Auction Company: Hong Kong Sotheby's
Date of Transaction: 2000-05-02

    This Cizhou Kiln pillow with tiger pattern is shaped like ruyi. The sides of the pillow are painted with weed patterns. The surface is painted with a plump, ferocious yet adorable tiger with medallion. The tiger is crouching on the ground and staring to the front as if having a rest. Beside the tiger, the grass is painted with just a few strokes. This porcelain of Cizhou Kiln is rich in patterns, including animals, flowers, figures, poems and opera scenes. It is a representative artwork of Cizhou Kiln pillows with tiger pattern.

Tri-color Silver Ingot-shaped Pillow

Origin: Song Dynasty

Length: 17.5 cm

Hammer Price: RMB 858,000

Name of Auction Company: Beijing Huachen

Date of Transaction: 2001-05-21

This pillow is shaped like an ingot with tri-color glaze, which looks like rosy clouds reflecting the sun. On the surface, a poem was inscribed in the fifty-third year of the Reign of Emperor Qianlong. The workmanship and the style of this pillow are similar to the inscriptions carved on the jadewares with neat characters. The cracked glaze of the tri-color pillow has not flaked off and the exquisite skill is rarely seen in history.

Ru Kiln Bowl with Patterns of Lotus Petal and Dragon

Origin: Song Dynasty
Height: 7.2 cm
Diameter of Mouth: 18.1 cm
Diameter of Bottom: 9.3 cm
Hammer Price: RMB 23,000,000
Name of Auction Company: Beijing Zhongjia
Date of Transaction: 2009-12-06

This bowl has an open mouth and an arc belly. Carved in the center are cloud and dragon patterns, and three layers of lotus patterns are carved in bas-relief on the ektexine with clear laminated layers. At the bottom the trace of sesame nail can be seen, which is rare in craftsmanship. It is exquisitely made with pure glaze and ice crazes and is regarded as a quality porcelain of Ru Kiln in the Song Dynasty.

Guan Kiln Gourd-shaped Bottle

Origin: Southern Song Dynasty

Height: 11 cm

Diameter of Mouth: 2.3 cm

Diameter of Foot: 3.9 cm

Hammer Price: RMB 1,320,000

Name of Auction Company: Shandong Jinghongtang

Date of Transaction: 2005-08-28

This gourd-shaped bottle has a straight mouth, a flat bottom and a round foot. This contracted waist gourd bottle consists of two parts with the smaller one on the top and the bigger one underneath. It is originally and uniquely shaped. The body of the bottle is fully painted with grayish-cyan ceramic glaze. The crackings of the glaze are tiny and dense with purplish black body, including the rim and the foot, hence the name "the purple mouth and the iron foot".

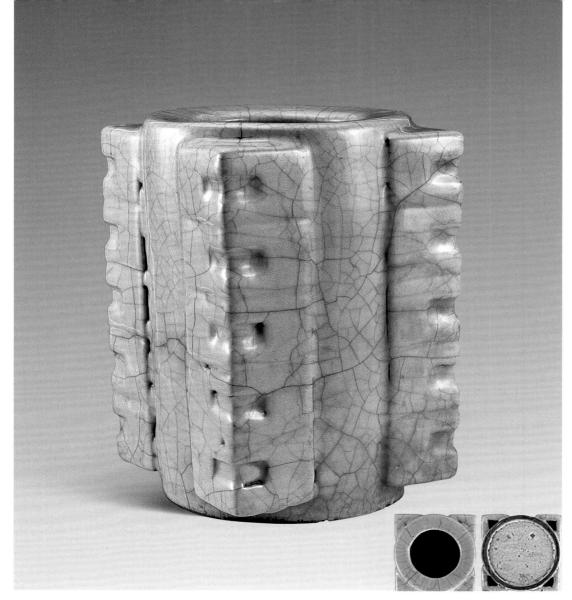

Guan Kiln Bottle in the Shape of Cong

Origin: Southern Song Dynasty
Height: 19.5 cm
Hammer Price: RMB 16,500,000
Name of Auction Company: Beijing Hanhai
Date of Transaction: 2006-06-26

This Guan Kiln bottle in the shape of cong is modeled after the shape of yucong in the Neolithic Age. This cong-style bottle has a round mouth, a short neck, a round foot and a square column-shaped body with concavo-convex patterns. It is fully painted with cracking cyan glaze, fine and smooth in texture. It is a treasured artwork from the imperial kilns of the Song Dynasty.

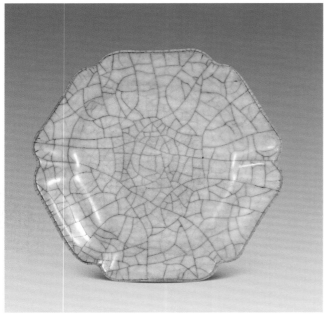

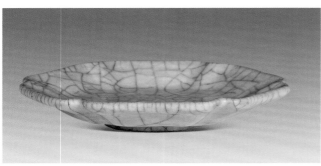

Ge Kiln Sunflower-shaped Plate

Origin: Southern Song Dynasty
Diameter of Mouth: 14.5 cm
Height: 2.8 cm
Diameter of Foot: 5.5 cm
Hammer Price:
RMB 2,860,000
Name of Auction Company:
Shanghai Jiatai
Date of Transaction:
2006-06-29

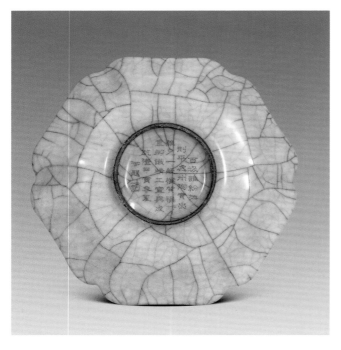

This Ge Kiln sunflower-shaped plate is pale yellow, elegantly carved and deftly made with finger marks, a fine blank and a round foot. The body is in the color of pale black with a natural form. This sunflower-shaped plate has fine material and thick glaze which is lenitive with crisp luster and a good sense of jade texture. The glaze starts from the surface of the body with irregular crackings, showing the colors of black and yellow, also known as "golden thread and iron line". The sound is deep when being knocked. The small work is equipped with big crackings. The cracking of the inner surface of the plate is fragmentized and the outer surface is decorated with crab-claw patterns. With two kinds of crackings on one vessel, it is really rare in Ge Kiln porcelain.

Longquan Dreg Pot

Origin: Southern Song Dynasty
Diameter of Mouth: 13.5 cm
Height: 9.8 cm
Hammer Price: RMB 495,000
Name of Auction Company: Shanghai Jiatai
Date of Transaction: 2006-12-03

This Longquan dreg pot has a trumpet-shaped mouth, a straight neck, a flat and round belly and a round foot. The color of the body is white and the pot is painted with cyan glaze. There is a red line on the joint of the glaze and the body. The circular base is bare without painting. This pot is used to hold food dregs. A person from the Yuan Dynasty wrote, "In the Song Dynasty, when the big clans host a banquet, bottles and vessels for the dregs of food must be used." The glaze of the article is slight with sky cyan. The article is big in size but thin, which is regarded as a fine article. Similar articles were unearthed from a Song Dynasty tomb in Dongxi, Jianyang County in 1974.

Green Glazed Flat Bottle

Origin: Liao Dynasty
Height: 12.5 cm
Appraisal: RMB 120,000
Name of Auction Company: Shanghai Changcheng
Date of Transaction: 2005-06-23

This green glazed flat bottle is oval narrow on the top and wide at the bottom. On the top of the bottle stand a circular rope-shaped handle, a straight mouth and leather strips on the base. There are two bumps on both sides of the belly, modeled after a metal rivet. The green glaze is not painted all over and the glaze is glittering and translucent with little crackings.

Tri-color Mandarin-duck-shaped Kettle

Origin: Liao Dynasty

Height: 18.2 cm

Appraisal: RMB 40,000

Name of Auction Company: Shanghai Changcheng

Date of Transaction: 2005-06-23

This tri-color mandarin-duck-shaped kettle is shaped like a floating mandarin duck. There is a lotus-shaped bowl on its back. The leaves and branches are linked to an annular handle. The mandarin duck is vivid and lively with a raised head and bulged eyes. The feathers are thick and arranged in tiers with distinctive grain. The hollow beak is used as the spout of the kettle, which is painted with yellow, green and white glaze, but not to the bottom. The glaze of the unpainted part of the body is beige and seems a little bit of running. This tri-color mandarin-duck-shaped kettle is the utensil of the Qidan nationality of the Liao Dynasty inhabiting northern China.

Black Glazed and Double-ear Flat Bottle Carved with Deer Pattern

Origin: Western Xia Dynasty

Height: 26 cm

Length: 10 cm

Appraisal: RMB 380,000

Name of Auction Company: Zhongpai International

Date of Transaction: 2006-05-20

This black glazed double-ear flat bottle carved with deer pattern has a small mouth, two ears, a round body, a flat belly and a round foot. There are curved brims near the rim. The two ears are wide and thick with several ridges. The belly is decorated with wave patterns. The glaze is evenly painted and it is pure. The lines of the engraved flower are smooth and gentle with deer, flower and grass patterns. The limbs of the deer are slender and nimble, and its head turns back with a flower in its mouth. This bottle is a typical product of the Lingwu Kiln of the Western Xia Dynasty.

Name: Brown Glazed Cocoon-shaped Bottle Incised with Fish Patten

Origin: Western Xia Dynasty

Height: 24 cm

Appraisal: RMB 280,000

Name of Auction Company: Zhongpai International

Date of Transaction: 2006-05-20

    This brown glazed and cocoon-shaped bottle incised with fish pattern is like a cocoon. It has a straight mouth with a circular lip. Two diamonds with medallion are engraved on the surface of the bottle, which is decorated with fish and alga patterns. The white blank and the black glaze set each other off. The pattern is evidently convex, thus acquiring the effect of bas-relief. The fish is agile and tough, and the line of the flower is natural, bold, smooth and stretching, which shows the style of simple and bold nomads. The upper and the lower sides of the bottle are decorated with string patterns and the blank is revealed on the base, which are the characteristics of the Lingwu Kiln of the Western Xia Dynasty. Medallion and fish patterns were also common decorations of that time.

Jun Kiln Sky Blue Open Vase Dotted with Purple Spots

Origin: Jin Dynasty
Height: 27.2 cm
Appraisal: RMB 10,000,000
Name of Auction Company: Hong Kong Christie's
Date of Transaction: 2002-10-28

    This sky blue open vase dotted with purple spots has an open mouth, an elongated neck, a drooping belly and a round foot. The sky blue milk mixed glaze is thick with purplish red spots on the rim and the belly. The shape is delicate and exquisite. The fresh pleasant sky blue glaze and the thick imposing rosy purple kiln spots are just like red rose petals falling from the blue sky in late autumn.

Jun Kiln Purplish Red Glazed Vase with Edges on Four Sides

Origin: Jin Dynasty

Height: 29.5 cm   Diameter: 23 cm   Diameter of Foot: 18 cm

Hammer Price: RMB 2,178,000

Name of Auction Company: Tianjin Emperor's Ferry

Date of Transaction: 2006-06-21

This Jun Kiln purplish red glazed vase with edges on four sides is a titbit collected by Japan's Izu Kogen Art Museum. The shape of the vase is modeled after the style of ancient bronzewares, with a trumpet-shaped mouth, a flat and bulged belly and a sloping round foot. The neck, belly and foot are affixed with edges, commonly known as "vase with edges on four sides". A variety of flowerpots and flowerpot bases are common in the porcelain of Jun Kiln passed down from the Song Dynasty. However, vases with edges are rare and precious.

Name: Yaozhou Kiln Bowl with Lotus Pattern

Origin: Jin Dynasty

Diameter: 18.7 cm

Hammer Price: RMB 27,500

Name of Auction Company: China Guardian

Date of Transaction: 2006-11-22

    This Yaozhou Kiln bowl with lotus pattern has an open mouth, an arc wall, a deep belly and a small round foot. The part below the mouth is decorated with a circle of string patterns. On the base there are some light brown spots due to oxidation. On the foot there are traces of sticky sand. The bowl is fully painted with cyan glaze mixed with a little yellow. In the bowl a group of lotuses are engraved. The line is smooth and natural with the effect of bas-relief.

V. Pottery and Porcelain of the Yuan Dynasty

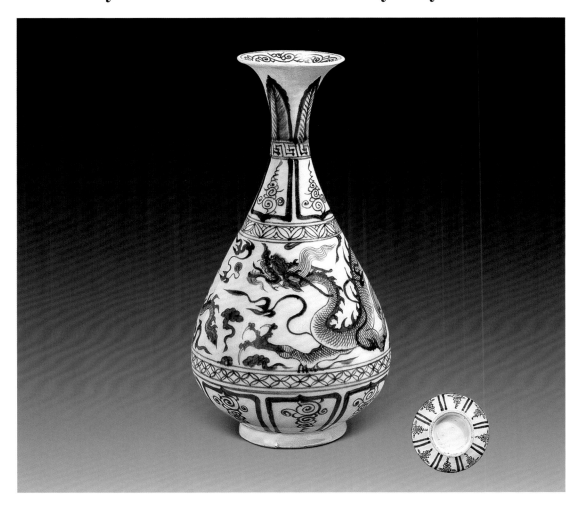

Blue-and-white Vase with Dragon and Pearl Patterns

Origin: Yuan Dynasty

Height: 28.5 cm   Hammer Price: RMB 781,000

Name of Auction Company: Yunnan Diancang

Date of Transaction: 2004-05-30

This bottle has a wide mouth, a thin neck, a bulged belly and a round foot. The whole body is embellished with blue-and-white decorations. There are curved grass motifs on the inner rim and three layers of patterns on its neck, namely, banana leave pattern, fret pattern and deformed lotus petal pattern. The main body of its belly is adorned with a dragon among the cloud motifs, with coin motifs on the upper and the lower sides. And its shin is adorned with deformed lotus petal patterns. The dragon pattern is strong and vigorous, and the vivid dragon is long and thin, playing with a treasured pearl. The vase is slender and graceful, representing the high artistic value of blue-and-white porcelain in the Yuan Dynasty.

Blue-and-white Pot with Pattern of "Guigu Descending the Mountains"

Origin: Yuan Dynasty
Diameter: 33 cm
Hammer Price:
RMB 228,618,086
Name of Auction Company:
London Christie's
Date of Transaction:
2005-07-12

This pot has a straight mouth, a short neck, a thick lip, a round shoulder, a bulged belly and a round foot. The whole body is embellished with a blue-and-white glaze, the rim is painted with seawater patterns, its shoulder is adorned with twining peony patterns, the belly is ornamented with the pattern of "Guigu Descending the Mountains", and the foot is decorated with deformed lotus petal patterns consisting of miscellaneous treasure patterns. The blue-and-white porcelain is embellished in a bright-colored way; the picture is painted in a meticulous way, making the subject matter and the background set off each other, thus constituting an integral whole. The figures on the pot are carved smoothly and naturally with vivid expressions.

Blue-and-white Pot with Patterns of Pine, Bamboo and Plum

Origin: Yuan Dynasty
Diameter: 22.9 cm
Hammer Price: RMB 22,684,000
Name of Auction Company:
Hong Kong Christie's
Date of Transaction: 2006-05-30

This pot has a straight mouth, a short neck, a plump shoulder, a bulged belly and a round foot. The whole body is embellished with white glaze, the rim is adorned with seawater patterns, the shoulder is painted with a circle of miscellaneous treasure patterns, its belly is ornamented with patterns of deer, magpie, plum, pine, bamboo and travertine, etc, meaning "the deer and the pine enjoying the spring season", "great joy and happiness", and its gaskin is embellished with a circle of lotus petal patterns. It is painted vividly and enameled in a green and lively way with delicate blank and smooth glaze. "The three friends in winter" refers to three kinds of plants, namely, pine, bamboo and plum, for they are well known for keeping their great vitality in the severe cold winter, symbolizing the lofty character and faithful friendship in traditional Chinese culture.

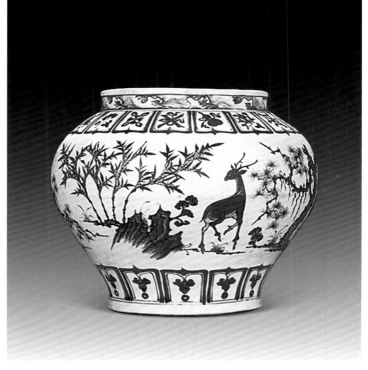

Blue-and-white Jar with Animal-shaped Ears and Patterns of Cloud, Dragon and Pearl

Origin: Yuan Dynasty
Height:39 cm
Hammer Price: RMB 10,158,775
Name of Auction Company: Hong Kong Christie's
Date of Transaction: 2003-10-27

This jar has a straight mouth, a long neck, an inclined broad shoulder, a bulged belly and a short round foot. On its shoulders are a pair of parallel animal ears. The whole body is embellished with six layers of blue-and-white patterns, curved grass pattern on the rim, twining lotus pattern on its neck, a circle of twining peony patterns on its shoulder, cloud and dragon patterns on its belly, a circle of half-coin patterns below its belly and a circle of lotus petal pattern at its bottom. The jar is shaped in a dignified way with graceful and exquisite patterns. The glaze is mainly blue with purple. Distinctive iron rust can be seen where it was brightly colored, which is the typical color of cobalt material. This article is regarded as a masterpiece of the blue-and-white porcelain of the Yuan Dynasty.

Blue-and-white Incense Burner with Flower Pattern

Origin: Yuan Dynasty
Dimension: 15.5 cm X 12 cm
Hammer Price: RMB 121,000
Name of Auction Company: Tianjin Emperor's Ferry
Date of Transaction: 2004-11-18

This incense burner has a round mouth, a short neck, two ears attached to the rim and its neck, a round bulged belly and a tripod. The whole body is embellished with four tiers of blue-and-white patterns from the top to the bottom, the rim is painted with flower pattern, its neck with curved grass pattern, its shoulders with tapestry pattern, its belly with twining chrysanthemum pattern and its shoulders inscribed with a single line of six regular script characters meaning "Made in the Eleventh Year of the Reign of Emperor Zhizheng". It is steady with fine quality. The white glaze has green color on it, the layer of the pattern is clear, the painting is smooth and unrestrained, and the blue-and-white ware is gray blue. It is considered as a product made in private kilns of Jingdezhen.

Red and Green Colored Lidded Pot with Patterns of Lotus Pond and Mandarin Duck

Origin: Yuan Dynasty

Height: 12.5 cm

Diameter of Mouth: 6.2 cm

Appraisal: RMB 100,000

Name of Auction Company: Zhongpai International

Date of Transaction: 2006-05-20

This pot has a straight neck, a plump shoulder, a round bulged belly, a short round foot and a lid. On its shoulders and belly is a circle of embossing joint trace. The lid is in a rhombus shape and red glaze is painted with double circles of string patterns and tendril patterns with its middle part bulged out. The button-like center embellished in green glaze is very eye-catching. The shoulder is ornamented with grass pattern in red glaze. The belly is painted with pond and mandarin duck patterns, on which there are two mandarin ducks swimming in the pond, with the male in the front looking backward at the female and both of them looking at each other, creating a cozy atmosphere. On its gaskin the jar is red-glazed in deformed lotus petal patterns with the white glaze mixed with green, which is elegant and smooth. The red and green glazes form a delightful contrast. The red and green porcelain is rarely seen in the Yuan Dynasty. It is best preserved and regarded as a classical work for its shape, glaze and colored painting.

Jizhou Kiln Colored Incense Burner with Surging Wave Pattern

Origin: Yuan Dynasty
Height: 18.6 cm
Diameter of Mouth: 19.6 cm
Diameter of Foot: 17.6 cm
Appraisal: RMB 600,000
Name of Auction Company: Zhongpai International
Date of Transaction: 2006-05-20

This incense burner is made up of two parts, but there are imitations which are siamesed. The upper part is embellished with surging wave pattern. The lower part is ornamented with geometric decorations, such as deformed fret pattern, bowstring pattern, etc, which is trenchant and unrestrained and forms a natural one. It is deemed as a rare treasure of underglaze paintings in the Yuan Dynasty. Most of the fine artworks of underglaze paintings of Jizhou Kiln are now found abroad, with a few of them collected in Jiangxi Museum.

Longquan Kiln Green Glazed Flat Bottle

Origin: Yuan Dynasty
Height: 31.5 cm
Hammer Price: RMB 429,000
Name of Auction Company: Zhongpai International
Date of Transaction: 2006-09-24

This bottle has a small slightly outward-sloping mouth, a short neck, a flat square belly, a wide shoulder and a narrow bottom. It has four ears, two on the shoulders and two near the bottom. The frame, embellished with two protruding bowstring patterns, is shaped like the Chinese character "亞". The center of the frame is decorated with a bas-relief dragon pattern, and its four corners are adorned with floating cloud patterns. The whole body, blue glazed, translucent and smooth, is a typical rare porcelain of Longquan Kiln. In the Yuan Dynasty, Longquan Kiln flourished. The scale of Longquan celadon production expanded and the quantity of kilns and products reached to an unprecedented level with a large variety of products of various styles. Many products were exported to other countries of the world.

Longquan Kiln Plate Carved with Pattern of Flying Dragon

Origin: Yuan Dynasty
Diameter: 36 cm
Hammer Price: RMB 451,000
Name of Auction Company: China Guardian
Date of Transaction: 2005-05-13

    This plate has a folded rim, an arc belly and a short round foot. The whole body is blue glazed, and the center of it is modeled with a tri-clawed imposing dragon playing with a fire pearl in auspicious clouds. The whole body is plump and smoothly glazed. The plate was specially made to suit Yuan Dynasty local Islamic noblemen for eating with their hands. A similar article is housed in the Topkapi Museum of Turkey, and fragments have been unearthed in Gao'an of Jiangxi Province. It is a rare treasure in that the center of its inner bottom is carved with a dragon pattern.

Blue Glazed Gilded Kettle

Origin: Yuan Dynasty
Height: 26.6 cm
Hammer Price: RMB 33,000,000
Name of Auction Company: Jiangyang Futong
Date of Transaction: 2006-09-16

This kettle has a washer-shaped mouth, a contracted neck, a flat round belly and a round foot. The glaze is soft sapphire and the body is gilded with banana leaf pattern, seawater pattern, dragon pattern and bowstring pattern. On one side of its belly, the dragon stretches its tongue and on the other side of the belly, the dragon curls its tail and hunches its back. On both sides in the middle, a peach-shaped area is polished and painted with a dragon in cloud pattern. The whole body is regular, steady, fine and smooth, and the soft sapphire glaze is translucent and smooth. It is quite precious because there are now a very limited number of existing gilded items of the Yuan Dynasty.

Blue Glazed Vase with White Dragon Pattern

Origin: Yuan Dynasty

Height: 24.5 cm

Hammer Price: RMB 2,750,000

Name of Auction Company: Beijing Hanhai

Date of Transaction: 2000-12-11

This vase has a small mouth, a short neck, a plump shoulder, a bulged belly and a round foot. The whole body is blue glazed with heavy and smooth glaze. The belly is carved with white dragon pattern, and the blue and the white colors set each other off. It is gracefully and elegantly shaped with a great artistic appeal. The decoration of blue glaze and white flower traces back to the Yuan Dynasty, that is, the pattern was modeled by incising, stacking, inlaying, and then white glaze was filled in, in such a way that the pattern not only had stereo perception, but also the blue-and-white color added radiance and beauty to each other in sharp contrast.

Jiexiu Kiln Brown Glazed Drinking Vessel Carved with Flower Pattern

Origin: Yuan Dynasty
Height: 77.5 cm
Hammer Price: RMB 980,500
Name of Auction Company: Hong Kong Christie's
Date of Transaction: 2001-04-30

This vessel has a petal-shaped mouth decorated with treasured beads to symbolize water drops, and a contracted neck. Both sides of the neck are adorned with pierced curved grass. It has also a round bulged belly and a trumpet-shaped high round foot. The whole body is brown glazed, and on its belly are two layers of brown glaze decorations. The upper part is adorned with lotus pattern and the bottom is carved with the honeysuckle pattern. On its round foot are the Chinese characters indicating the craftsman and the time of making. This is a very rare treasure because it is a representative item of Jiexiu Kiln, which combines incising with piercing.

Underglaze Red Vase with Pattern of Medallion Lotus Pond

Origin: Yuan Dynasty

Length: 45.5 cm

Diameter of Mouth: 5.7 cm

Diameter of Bottom: 13.5 cm

Hammer Price: RMB 1,609,650

Name of Auction Company: Macau Chung Shun

Date of Transaction: 2009-08-22

This underglaze red vase has a small mouth, a flat rim, a short slender neck, a plump shoulder and a round foot. Painted all over it are underglaze red patterns on white ground. On its shoulders are three layers of patterns, from top to bottom, namely, patterns of curved grass, patterns of twining lotus and pattern of fretwork. This vase is decorated around its belly with patterns of mandarin ducks beside the graceful lotus. There are decorative patterns of curved grass and patterns of deformed lotus flower at its lower end. The fine and pure blank, elegant and exquisite form and style make this vase a typical item of underglaze red porcelain of Jingdezhen kilns of the Yuan Dynasty.

Blue-and-white Underglaze Red Pot with Twining Peony Pattern

Origin: Yuan Dynasty
Height: 23.5 cm
Diameter of Mouth: 15 cm
Diameter of Bottom: 16 cm
Hammer Price: RMB 5,900,000
Name of Auction Company: Beijing Zhongjia
Date of Transaction: 2009-12-06

This blue-and-white underglaze red pot has a labial mouth, a short neck, a sloping shoulder, a bulged belly and a round foot with the blank exposed. It is decorated around its neck with patterns of curved grass and patterns of twining lotus around its shoulders. There are twining peony patterns around the belly. The branches and leaves are applied with blue-and-white glaze, and the front, flank and back sides of the plum in full blossom are applied with underglaze red. Near the foot is deformed lotus petal design. This pot has the characteristics of regular and exquisite form and style, and lustrous and smooth glaze.

VI. Pottery and Porcelain of the Ming Dynasty

Underglaze Red Melon Edge Pot with Patterns of Branch and Flower

Origin: Reign of Emperor Hongwu of the Ming Dynasty
Height: 35 cm
Hammer Price: RMB 4,140,900
Name of Auction Company: Hong Kong Christie's
Date of Transaction: 1999-04-26

    This underglaze red melon edge pot has an outward-sloping mouth, a short neck, a plump shoulder, a bulged belly and a round foot, with no inscription or glaze on the exterior of the bottom. Painted all over are underglaze red decorative patterns on white ground with 10 layers of decorative patterns on the exterior. There are fretwork pattern and pattern of ruyi cloud. There are finely modeled pattern of deformed twining lotus petal, pattern of whitish cloud and patterns of ruyi cloud motifs with twining lotus. This pot is decorated on the belly with patterns of 12 groups of flowers of four seasons, together with lake stones. In the lower part of the pot are three layers of decorative patterns, namely, from top to bottom, pattern of deformed lotus petals with the design of twining chrysanthemum blossom, fretwork pattern, pattern of deformed twining lotus petal and pattern of curved grass on the foot.

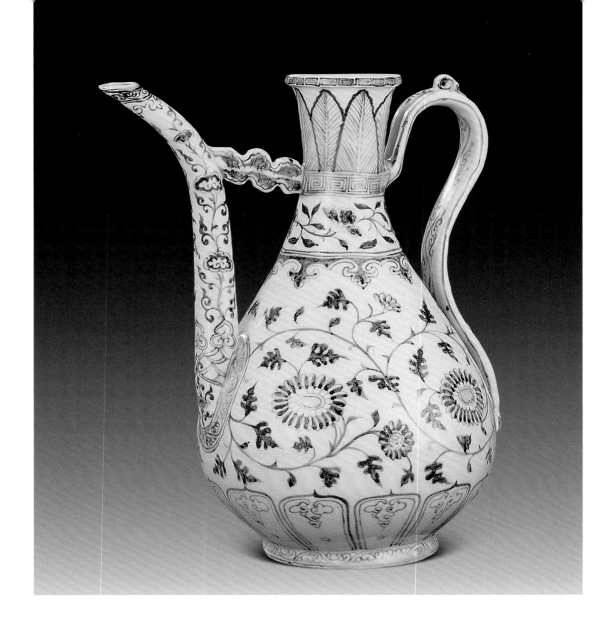

Blue-and-white Kettle with Pattern of Twining Chrysanthemum

Origin: Reign of Emperor Hongwu of the Ming Dynasty

Height: 32.5 cm   Hammer Price: RMB 10,812,000

Name of Auction Company: Hong Kong Christie's   Date of Transaction: 2005-11-28

This blue-and-white kettle has a labial mouth, a long slender neck, a sloping shoulder, a bulged belly and a round foot. The body of this kettle has the same design as jade wine vessels. On one side of the body is a long slender spout with a cloud-shaped ornament. On the other side is a bent handle with a small ear, connecting the neck and the belly. Painted all over are blue-and-white decorative patterns with fretwork pattern around the rim. Around the neck, from top to bottom, are pattern of banana leaf, fretwork pattern, pattern of twining ganoderma and pattern of ruyi cloud motif. There are pattern of twining chrysanthemum on its belly, lotus petal pattern near the foot, and twining flower patterns on the spout and the handle. The round foot is decorated with the white glazed pattern of curved grass.

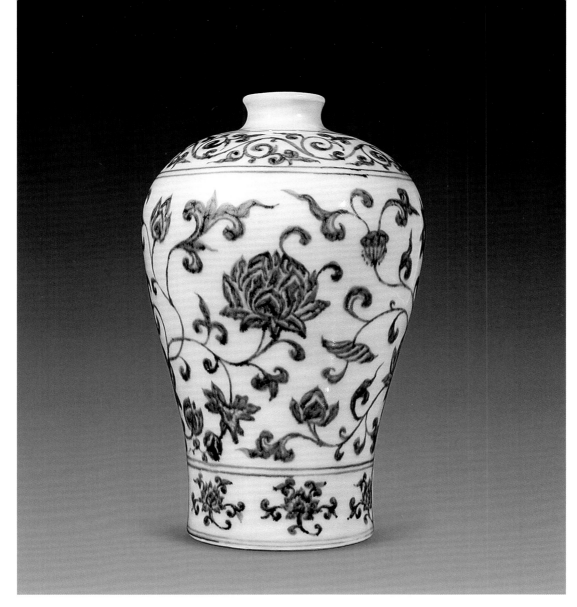

Blue-and-white Vase with Pattern of Twining Lotus

Origin: Reign of Emperor Yongle of the Ming Dynasty
Height: 24.8 cm
Hammer Price: RMB 1,980,000
Name of Auction Company: Beijing Council
Date of Transaction: 2006-11-23

    This blue-and-white vase has a small labial mouth, a short neck, a plump shoulder and a wide round foot with the blank exposed. Painted all over are blue-and-white decorative patterns on white ground. This vase is decorated on the shoulder with curving grass pattern, with twining lotus design on the body and bended lotus branch pattern in the lower part. The regular and exquisite form and style, pure white blank, fine workmanship and skillfully blue-and-white decorating workmanship make this vase a precious imperial utensil of great value produced in Jingdezhen imperial kilns in the Reign of Emperor Hongwu of the Ming Dynasty.

Blue-and-white Kettle with Pattern of Medallion Twining Flower

Origin: Reign of Emperor Yongle of the Ming Dynasty

Height: 35.9 cm

Hammer Price: RMB 10,154,800

Name of Auction Company: Hong Kong Sotheby's

Date of Transaction: 2002-05-07

This blue-and-white kettle (the lid is missing) has a straight mouth, a long slender neck, a bent shoulder, a long belly and a round foot. On one side is a handle, and on the other side is a spout in a cucurbit shape. Painted all over are blue-and-white decorative patterns on white ground. There are twining flower pattern on the neck, lotus petal design on the shoulders and curved grass pattern on the foot. Its belly is decorated with octal rectangular medallions, each of which is decorated with two flowers.

Blue-and-white Ribbon-shaped-eared Flat Bottle with Pattern of Twining Lotus

Origin: Reign of Emperor Yongle of the Ming Dynasty
Hammer Price:
RMB 20,487,500
Name of Auction Company:
Hong Kong Christie's
Date of Transaction: 2007-11-27

This blue-and-white ribbon-shaped-eared flat bottle has a garlic-shaped mouth, a contracted neck, a flat and round belly, and bi-shaped foot, with no inscription. Painted all over are blue-and-white decorative patterns on white ground. There are two symmetric ribbon-shaped ears connecting the mouth.

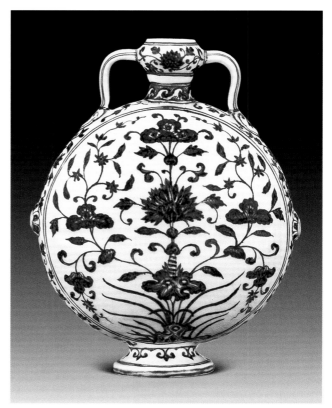

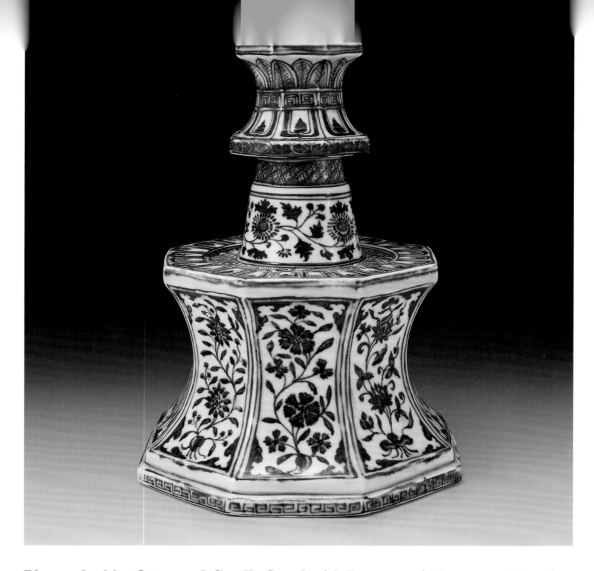

Blue-and-white Octagonal Candle Stand with Patterns of Flower and Bending Branch

Origin: Reign of Emperor Yongle of the Ming Dynasty

Height: 29.8 cm   Hammer Price: RMB 20,350,000

Name of Auction Company: Beijing Hanhai   Date of Transaction: 2005-06-20

This blue-and-white octagonal candle stand has a candle holder, a connecting column and a base. The upright column connects the holder with the base. With a hollow interior, the base is used for holding the guttering of candles. Painted all over are blue-and-white decorative patterns on white ground. The candle holder is decorated, from top to bottom, with the pattern of banana leaf, fretwork pattern and deformed lotus petal design. There are tapestry pattern and bended branch design on the column, seawater and lotus petal patterns around the base and fretwork pattern on the foot. On each of the eight sides is decorated with medallions with various patterns of twining flower. Sulima blue, an imported cobalt material for glazing and decoration, makes blue-and-white patterns lustrous and glossy. The novel and exquisite design, elegant and regular form and style, and gorgeous decorative pattern make this candle stand a masterpiece.

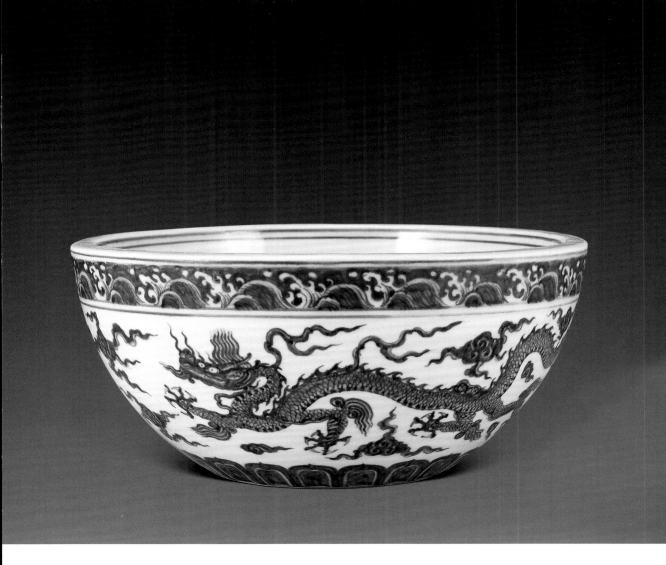

Blue-and-white Bowl with Cloud and Dragon Patterns

Origin: Reign of Emperor Xuande of the Ming Dynasty
Diameter: 26.7 cm
Hammer Price: RMB 3,520,000
Name of Auction Company: Beijing Hanhai
Date of Transaction: 2006-12-18

This blue-and-white bowl is decorated with patterns of seawater near the rim, patterns of cloud and dragon on the belly and patterns of lotus petal towards the bottom. The inscription meaning"Made in the Reign of Emperor Xuande of the Ming Dynasty"is written inside the two blue-and-white circles on the inner bottom. The stocky and exquisite design, vivid decorative patterns and imposing dragon design make this bowl a masterpiece produced in kilns of the Reign of Emperor Xuande.

Pomegranate Flower Pattern Fruit Plate with White Flowers on Blue Ground

Origin: Reign of Emperor Xuande of the Ming Dynasty
Diameter: 29.5 cm
Hammer Price: RMB 17,120,000
Name of Auction Company: Hong Kong Sotheby's
Date of Transaction: 2007-04-08

This pomegranate flower pattern fruit plate has an open mouth, an arc inner wall and a round foot with the flint-red blank exposed. The exterior and the interior of this plate are decorated with white-glazed patterns of flower and fruit on diamond blue ground. There are patterns of pomegranate flower in the white circle at the center, patterns of flower and fruit of the four seasons on the interior wall and bended lotus design on the exterior wall, with the blue-glazed inscription of "Made in the Reign of Emperor Xuande of the Ming Dynasty" on the exterior near the rim. The regular form, thick clay, glossy and lustrous blue glaze, exquisite and vivid pattern make this fruit plate a precious blue-glazed porcelain on white ground in the Reign of Emperor Xuande.

Violet Gold Glazed Shadow Flower Bowl with Cloud and Dragon Patterns

Origin: Reign of Emperor Xuande of the Ming Dynasty

Diameter of Mouth: 21 cm

Hammer Price: RMB 3,960,000

Name of Auction Company: Shanghai Jiatai

Date of Transaction: 2005-06-05

This violet gold glazed shadow flower bowl has a slightly outward-sloping rim, a deep arc belly and a round foot. It is applied with dark red brown glaze all over. With the heads and tails linked up, a shape like a snake and looking covetously at the fire-pearls, two dragons, with open mouths, wide open eyes, swaying hairs, sharp wheel-like claws, which are full of power, grandeur, vigor and vitality, are incised indistinctly on the interior wall of this bowl, with pattern of ruyi cloud motifs at the bottom. With the crawling part a bit green, the exterior bottom is applied with white glaze with the inscription meaning "Made in the Reign of Emperor Xuande of the Ming Dynasty" at the bottom. The exquisite designed and elegant-looking bowl is a product of the imperial kilns in Jingdezhen in the Reign of Emperor Xuande in the Ming Dynasty.

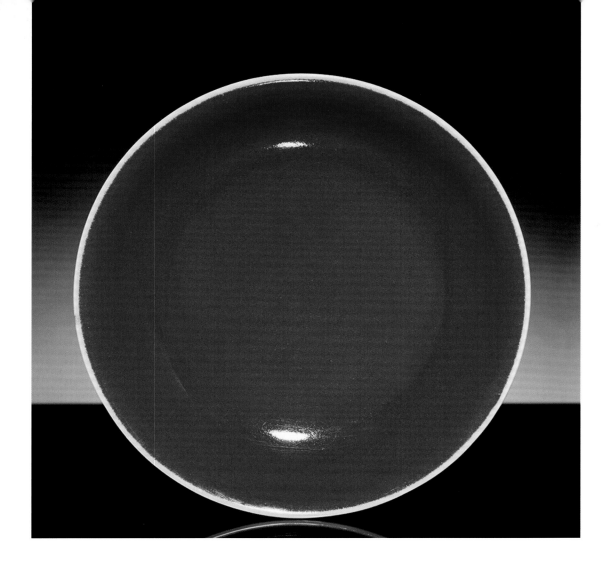

Red Glazed Plate

Origin: Reign of Emperor Xuande of the Ming Dynasty
Diameter: 20.2 cm
Hammer Price: RMB 6,209,200
Name of Auction Company: Hong Kong Christie's
Date of Transaction: 2010-12-01

This red glazed plate has an open mouth, an arc wall and a round foot. It is applied with red glaze all over. Melted at an extremely high temperature, the copper-red glaze on the rim makes its way down and the white blank exposed, which is commonly called rush-like rim. There is an inscription of "Made in the Reign of Emperor Xuande of the Ming Dynasty" written in two lines, decorated with blue-white patterns and carved in regular script on the round foot. The regular and exquisite form and style, uniformed and even layer, and gorgeous and splendid color make this plate a typical red glazed porcelain produced in the imperial kilns in the Reign of Emperor Xuande.

Blue-and-white Vase with Pattern of Visiting a Friend with a Zither

Origin: Reign of Emperor Zhengtong of the Ming Dynasty

Height: 32 cm   Hammer Price: RMB 649,000

Name of Auction Company: Nanjing Shizhuzhai

Date of Transaction: 2006-06-08

This blue-and-white vase has a small mouth, a short neck, plump shoulders, a bulged belly, a round foot with the blank exposed and a gritty bottom. Painted all over are blue-and-white decorative patterns on white ground. This vase is decorated on the shoulders and neck with blue-and-white pattern of twining lotus, banana leaf design in the lower part and blue-and-white patterns of figure, mountain, stone, tree and flowing cloud on the body, together with the pattern of visiting a friend with a zither. The overall composition of the patterns is elaborately arranged with a full sense of coherence and fine painting skills, with figures of great vigor, freedom and grace. With a bright lustrous color and thin blue-and-white patterns, this vase is full of interest and taste. The straight and elegant design, pure and exquisite blank, glossy, fine and classical glaze, vivid decoration, distinct arrangement, and vigorous painting skills make this vase a masterpiece.

Blue-and-white Bowl with Pomegranate Pattern

Origin: Reign of Emperor Chenghua of Ming Dynasty
Diameter: 13.2 cm
Hammer Price: RMB 6,820,000
Name of Auction Company: Beijing Hanhai
Date of Transaction: 2004-11-22

This blue-and-white bowl has an open mouth, an arc belly and a crouching foot. Painted all over are blue-and-white decorative patterns on white ground with the blue inscription of"Made in the Reign of Emperor Chenghua of the Ming Dynasty"on the exterior of the bottom. There is a carved sankrit on the interior of the bottom, curved grass design on the interior rim, fretwork pattern on the exterior rim, and pomegranate pattern on the exterior wall. With a slight blank and a light body, elegant and lustrous blue-and-white glaze, fine and slender decorative pattern, and natural, vivid and fresh painting, this bowl is a masterpiece of blue-and-white porcelain produced in the imperial kilns of the Reign of Emperor Chenghua of the Ming Dynasty.

Clashing Color Pot with Cloud and Dragon Patterns and the Chinese Character"Tian"(Heaven) Written on the Outer Bottom

Origin: Reign of Emperor Chenghua of the Ming Dynasty

Height: 11.5 cm

Diameter of Mouth: 6.4 cm

Diameter of Bottom: 8.6 cm

Hammer Price: RMB 6,160,000

Name of Auction Company: Beijing Zhongjia

Date of Transaction: 2010-05-09

This clashing color pot has a straight mouth, a sloping shoulder, a bulged belly, a round foot and a round lid. At the top of the lid and on the belly are decorative patterns of dragon and cloud, with deformed lotus petal designs around the shoulders and near the foot. There is a Chinese character"Tian"(heaven) inscribed on the outer bottom in blue-and-white glaze. Blue-and-white glazed dragon pattern, clashing color glazed cloud pattern and lotus petal design have the characteristics of exquisite painting and graceful lines.

Clashing color with Chicken Pattern

Origin: Ming Dynasty

Height: 3.8 cm

Diameter: 8.2 cm

Hammer Price: RMB 22,050,000

Name of Auction Company: Macau Chung Shun

Date of Transaction: 2009-08-22

This clashing color mug has a slightly outward-sloping rim, a bulged belly and a flat bottom. It is decorated on the exterior wall with the pattern of the natural scenery of early spring: two flocks of hens and chicks are wandering among lake-stones, Chinese roses and tranquil orchids, with no glaze around the foot and with the blue inscription of "Made in the Reign of Emperor Chenghua of the Ming Dynasty" at the center of the bottom. This clashing color with chicken pattern is a typical design of clashing color porcelain in the Reign of Emperor Chenghua, which is of great value and is recorded repeatedly in the historical documents of the Ming and Qing Dynasties.

Yellow Glazed Blue-and-white Plate with Flower and Fruit Patterns

Origin: Reign of Emperor Hongzhi of the Ming Dynasty

Diameter: 26.3 cm

Hammer Price: RMB 2,310,000

Name of Auction Company: Beijing Hanhai

Date of Transaction: 2006-06-26

This yellow glazed blue-and-white plate has an outward-sloping mouth, an arc wall, a slightly sunken center and a round foot. Painted all over are blue-and-white decorative patterns on yellow ground. There are bended gardenia pattern in the center, patterns of bended branches of auspicious fruits, such as pomegranate, cherry, lotus seedpod, grape on the interior wall, and twining peony design on the exterior wall, with the blue inscription of "Made in the Reign of Emperor Hongzhi of the Ming Dynasty" in the two circles of blue-and-white glaze of the exterior bottom.

Blue-and-white Ganoderma Five-peaked Brush Holder with Arabic Inscription

Origin: Reign of Emperor Zhengde of the Ming Dynasty

Length: 21.9 cm

Hammer Price: RMB 3,938,800

Name of Auction Company: Hong Kong Christie's

Date of Transaction: 2010-12-01

This writing brush holder, with a rectangular base, is shaped like five peaks, the middle of which protrudes slightly and the other peaks on both sides lowering down successively. It is decorated all over with blue-and-white and surrounded by tree branch and glossy ganoderma patterns. The bottom medallion of the middle peak is inscribed with the Arabic inscription meaning "brush" and "holder". The frame of the base is inscribed with "Made in the Reign of Emperor Zhengde of the Ming Dynasty" in regular script. As Emperor Zhengde worshipped and believed in Islamism, many porcelain of his reign were decorated with Arabic words with auspicious meanings, making it quite unique and special.

Five-color Square Plate with Flower and Butterfly Patterns

Origin: Reign of Emperor Jiajing of the Ming Dynasty

Diameter: 17.8 cm

Hammer Price: RMB 1,272,000

Name of Auction Company: Hong Kong Christie's

Date of Transaction: 2005-11-28

This square plate has a slightly outward-sloping mouth, an oblique belly and a flat bottom. It is carved all over in relief with blue-and-white polychromes. Carved in the center are travertine flowers and plants, and the medallions of walls are dragon designs, mixed with trellis designs. The outer bottom was engraved with two lines of Chinese characters in regular script which read "Made in the Reign of Emperor Jajing of the Ming Dynasty". With a neat and white design, fine texture and bright color, this plate conforms to the standard multicolored plates and represents the superb workmanship of porcelain making in the Reign of Emperor Jiajing.

Blue-and-white "Round Sky and Square Earth" Gourd-shaped Bottle With Figure Pattern

Origin: Reign of Emperor Jiajing of the Ming Dynasty
Height: 66 cm
Hammer Price:
RMB 1,078,000
Name of Auction Company:
Liaoning International
Date of Transaction:
2007-06-10

This bottle is shaped like a gourd. In Chinese, "gourd" is pronounced "hulu", with the same meanings as "blessing" and "annual pay given by the emperor". The round top and square bottom are the symbol of round sky and square earth. Decorated on the upper part are auspicious clouds, a red-crowned crane, and the god of longevity, who is riding a deer. On the neck of the vase is the Chinese character meaning "longevity".

Blue-and-white Inverted-bell-shaped Bowl with Goat Pattern (one pair)

Origin: Reign of Emperor Jiajing of the Ming Dynasty

Diameter: 16.5 cm   Height: 10.5 cm

Hammer Price: RMB 22,167,500

Name of Auction Company: Hong Kong Sotheby's

Date of Transaction: 2007-10-09

This pair of inverted-bell-shaped bowls are decorated all over with blue-and-white on white ground. Decorated on the interiors of the bowls are kylins and embellished with pines, stones, flowers and plants. Brocade patterns are painted on the inner rim and three goats different in expression and posture are standing on the outside wall. Among the goats are patterns of pine, bamboo, plum, willow and banana. There are two lines of Chinese characters in regular script on the outside bottom, which read "Made in the Reign of Emperor Jiajing of the Ming Dynasty". The white and fine texture, smooth glaze and bright colors are features of porcelain for the imperial palace.

Blue-and-white Jar with Patterns of Lotus Pond and Mandarin Duck

Origin: Reign of Emperor Longqing of the Ming Dynasty
Diameter: 49 cm
Hammer Price: RMB 154,000
Name of Auction Company: Liaoning International
Date of Transaction: 2006-06-17

This jar has a wide-rimmed labial mouth, a deep and arc belly and a large and flat bottom with flint red. There are patterns of cloud on the outer rim, a lotus pond and mandarin ducks on its belly, propitious clouds at the bottom and the inscription "Made in the Reign of Emperor Longqing of the Ming Dynasty". This jar is lustrous, smooth and pure-white, the decorative pattern is brief and finely textured, and the color of the blue-and-white glaze is rich and gaudy, which makes it a masterpiece of the Reign of Emperor Longqing.

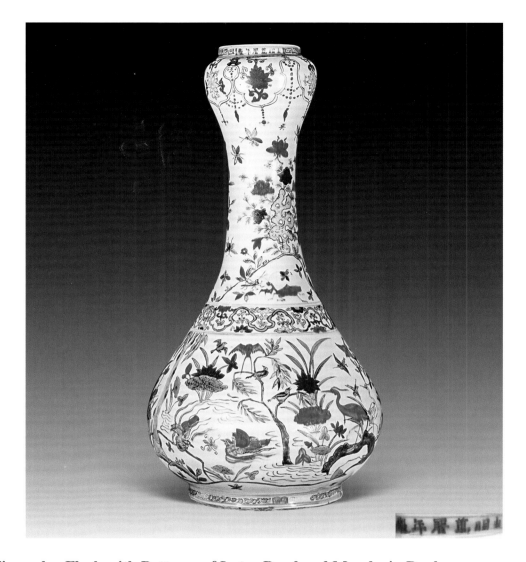

Five-color Flask with Patterns of Lotus Pond and Mandarin Duck

Origin: Reign of Emperor Wanli of the Ming Dynasty

Height: 53.9 cm

Hammer Price: RMB 7,264,000

Name of Auction Company: Hong Kong Sotheby's

Date of Transaction: 2007-04-08

With a garlic-shaped mouth, a long and thin neck, a bulged belly and a round foot, this flask is decorated all over with pained blue-and-white. The overglaze color is various, such as red, yellow, green, brown and purple. The three-layer decorations of the neck, from top to bottom, are patterns of flower, butterfy and cloud. The belly is mainly decorated with the patterns of pond and mandarin duck. Below the rim is the inscription in regular script which reads "Made in the Reign of Emperor Wanli of the Ming Dynasty". With dignified and elegant design, fine and exquisite decorative patterns, and smooth and fluent lines, this flask was used as a piece of imperial ornament.

Enamel Glazed Vase with Lotus Pond Pattern

Origin: Ming Dynasty in the 16th Century
Height: 38 cm
Hammer Price:
RMB 2,976, 480
Name of Auction Company:
Hong Kong Christie's
Date of Transaction:
2005-05-30

This vase has a labial mouth, a short neck, plump shoulders, a bulged belly and a round foot. It is decorated all over with enamel blue glaze. The decorative patterns of the shoulders are phoenix and ruyi cloud pattern. The principal emblazonry of the belly is lotus pond pattern and the lotuses are painted with yellow glaze. The gaskin is painted with seawater patterns. With neat and white design, fine texture and bright color, this article was a masterpiece in the Mid-Ming Dynasty.

Blue-and-white Animal-shaped-eared Drinking Vessel with Dragon and Phoenix Patterns

Origin: Reign of Emperor Wanli of the Ming Dynasty
Height: 94 cm
Hammer Price: RMB 3,850,000
Name of Auction Company: Beijing Hanhai
Date of Transaction: 2004-01-12

With an outward-sloping mouth, a long neck and a round foot, this vessel is decorated all over with blue-and-white glaze. The rim is painted with curved grass pattern and the neck, belly and bottom are painted with dragon and phoenix patterns. The three layers of decorations on the lower part of the neck are auspicious cloud, curved grass and wreath patterns. Below the rim is the inscription in regular script which reads "Made in the Reign of Emperor Wanli of the Ming Dynasty". This vessel is an official ornament, modeled after bronzewares in the Shang and Zhou Dynasties. The dragon and phoenix patterns symbolize auspiciousness and prosperity.

Blue-and-white Drinking Vessel with Flower Pattern Made under the Supervision of Mi Wanzhong

Origin: Reign of Emperor Tianqi of the Ming Dynasty
Height: 32 cm
Hammer Price: RMB 12,320, 000
Name of Auction Company:
Beijing Poly
Date of Transaction: 2010-12-05

This drinking vessel has an outward-sloping mouth, a long neck and a bulged belly. It is decorated all over with blue-and-white glaze, all sides of the neck are decorated with patterns of travertine and flowers in four seasons, the walls are decorated with flowers and plants, the lower part is painted with grape harvest picture, and the lower part of the neck and the area around the foot are each painted with a circle of banana leaf pattern. One side of the mouth is carved with a horizontal version of seven Chinese characters which read "Made under the Supervision of Mi Wanzhong in the Reign of Emperor Tianqi of the Ming Dynasty". This is a rare treasure as it is inscribed with the year of production.

Five-color Plate with Dragon Pattern

Origin: Reign of Emperor Chongzhen of the Ming Dynasty
Diameter of Mouth: 26.5 cm
Hammer Price: RMB 918,400
Name of Auction Company: Beijing Rongbao
Date of Transaction: 2010-11-14

  This plate has an open mouth, an arc belly and a round foot. The decorations are composed of a combination of colors of red, green, black, yellow and malachite green. A dragon pattern is painted in the center of the plate, the spine of which is in the shape of an awl. Around the dragon are sea waves, grotesque rocks and river cliffs. The exterior wall is painted with the patterns of two dragons playing with a pearl, flame and miscellaneous treasures. The bottom is inscribed with the blue-and-white inscription of "Made for Use at Mengzhao Mansion". The texture is hard and sturdy, and the line is smooth and fluent.

Shiwan Kiln Leaf-shaped Brush Washer

Origin: Ming Dynasty
Width: 25 cm
Hammer Price: RMB 190,400
Name of Auction Company: China Guardian
Date of Transaction: 2008-11-10

This brush washer is shaped like a leaf with upturned rim. The interior is carved with leaf veins. There are several flower buds engraved on the leaf stalk. It has three feet at the bottom and is decorated all over with glaze and full of fantasy, for we can see some white in the blue. The autumn leaf is exquisite and lifelike, and stretches beautifully. With the ingenious idea "When one leaf of Chinese parasol falls, all know that fall is here soon", it is really a brilliant article for the study room.

VII. Porcelain of the Qing Dynasty

Blue-and-white Plate with the Pattern of the Eight Immortals Celebrating the Birthday of Queen Mother of the West

Origin: Reign of Emperor Shunzhi of the Qing Dynasty

Diameter: 34.5 cm

Hammer Price: RMB 200,000

Name of Auction Company: Zhongding International

Date of Transaction: 2008-06-14

This plate has an open mouth, an arc wall, a flat bottom and a round foot. The rim is applied with brown glaze. It is decorated all over with blue-and-white glaze. Inside the plate is the pattern of the Eight Immortals celebrating the birthday of Queen Mother of the West. The Eight Immortals, in different postures, are holding different magic implements. The exterior bottom bears the inscription meaning "A Fine Article in the Jade Hall". This plate is featured by neat design, fine texture, bright colors and lifelike figures.

Blue-and-white Five-color Vase with Figures from Romance of the West Chamber

Origin: Reign of Emperor Shunzhi of the Qing Dynasty
Height: 39 cm
Hammer Price: RMB 198,000
Name of Auction Company: Beijing Council
Date of Transaction: 2006-04-22

This vase has an open mouth, a contracted neck, a sloping shoulder and a cylindrical belly. It is decorated all over with blue-and-white five-color patterns. On its neck is a circle of stones and twining flowers, on its whole body are figures of Romance of the West Chamber. The story of Romance of the West Chamber was widespread and craftsmen of Jingdezhen combined their exquisite skills with the fantastic story with lifelike figures, rich decorations and bright colors, creating the best visual effect. The color of this vase is similar to that of the traditional chinese ink paintings which are elegant and graceful and full of artistic charm. Inscribed with a poem and a prose, the figures on the vase are meticulous and true to life.

Blue-and-white Vase with Dragon Pattern

Origin: Reign of Emperor Kangxi of the Qing Dynasty
Height: 24.1 cm
Hammer Price: RMB 23,420,800
Name of Auction Company: Hong Kong Christie's
Date of Transaction: 2006-11-28

This vase has a slightly outward-sloping mouth, a short and thin neck, a round shoulder, a bulged belly and a round foot. It is painted with two imposing, powerful and ferocious dragons. On the outside bottom is the inscription in regular script meaning "Made in the Reign of Emperor Kangxi of the Qing Dynasty". It is straight and upright and is a fine blue-and-white porcelain made in the imperial kiln of that time.

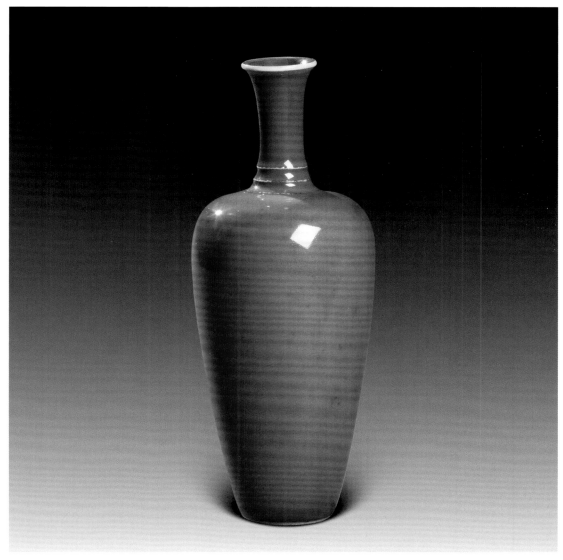

Cowpea Red Glazed Radish-shaped Vase

Origin: Reign of Emperor Kangxi of the Qing Dynasty
Height: 19.7 cm
Hammer Price: RMB 2,916,855
Name of Auction Company: Hong Kong Christie's
Date of Transaction: 2003-07-07

This vase has an outward-sloping mouth, a long and thin neck, a deep belly and a foot which is concave in the center. It is colored all over with cowpea red glaze. There are three circles of string patterns in the lower part of the neck. White blank can be seen below its neck owing to the thin glaze. The outside bottom is applied with white glaze with the regular script inscription "Made in the Reign of Emperor Kangxi of the Qing Dynasty". Among all the creative radish-shaped vases in the Reign of Emperor Kangxi of the Qing Dynasty, this one is a fine product for its uniform and graceful color.

Five-color Plate with Flower and Bird Patterns

Origin: Reign of Emperor Kangxi of the Qing Dynasty
Diameter: 19.5 cm
Hammer Price: RMB 495,000
Name of Auction Company: China Guardian
Date of Transaction: 2001-04-25

This plate has an open mouth, a bulged belly and a round foot. It is decorated all over with five-color glaze. The interior of the plate are decorated with hiden dragon and cloud patterns under the glaze, and there are hiden lotus and flower patterns on the inner wall of the plate. On the interior of the plate, flowers, birds and fruits are brightly carved with five-color glaze on white glaze. There are four Chinese seal-script characters in the centre of the plate meaning "unbounded happiness". The quality is fine and smooth and the painting is of exquisite skill. This plate is considered as an especially treasured article produced in the imperial kiln in Jingdezhen.

Five-color Lidded Bowl with Bat and Peach (Symbols of Happiness and Longevity) Pattern

Origin: Reign of Emperor Kangxi of the Qing Dynasty
Diameter: 12.7 cm   Hammer Price: RMB 298,920
Name of Auction Company: Hong Kong Christie's
Date of Transaction: 2000-10-31

This bowl has an outward-sloping mouth, a bulged belly and a round foot. It is decorated with five-color glaze, the outside wall of the bowl is adorned with a circle of twining clouds and pearls, and on the main body of its belly are five peaches and a bat, meaning in Chinese"prolonged longevity and great blessings". It is graceful and elegant with fine and smooth quality, the white glaze is sturdy and compact, and the five-color is beautiful and bright. It is much more exquisite than other porcelain treasures of that time and it is guessed that it may have been made in the imperial kiln in Jingdezhen in the 52nd year of the Reign of Emperor Kangxi as a gift for the 60th birthday of Emperor Kangxi.

Enamel Colored Cup with Patterns of Chinese Rose and Bamboo and Poem Inscription

Origin: Reign of Emperor Yongzheng of the Qing Dynasty
Diameter: 6.2 cm
Hammer Price: RMB 19,088,800
Name of Auction Company: Hong Kong Christie's
Date of Transaction: 1999-04-26

  This enamel colored cup has an open mouth, an arc belly and a flat bottom. The whole cup is decorated with white enamel glaze, bamboo and Chinese rose are painted on the body in various shades of colors, and flowers are drawn in layers of bright colors and beautiful red glaze. The vivid bamboos and blooming flowers present a miraculous picture. In the blank space of this picture, the verse "Branches are lush for a long time" is written in ink color. There are four Chinese characters on the outside bottom meaning "Made in the Reign of Emperor Yongzheng of the Qing Dynasty" in blue regular script. The blank is fine and white, and the cup is cute and exquisite. It is extremely precious, as articles of this kind are very rarely found nowadays.

Double-ear Vase with Famille Rose Peony Pattern on Coral Red Ground

Origin: Reign of Emperor Yongzheng of the Qing Dynasty
Height: 31.8 cm
Hammer Price: RMB 7,920,000
Name of Auction Company: China Guardian
Date of Transaction: 2006-06-03

This vase has a straight mouth, a thick straight neck, a sloping shoulder and a round foot. The belly is olive-shaped, and its shin is bended slightly. There are a pair of symmetrical ears on each side of the neck, and two rectangle holes near the foot. The whole body is painted with coral red as the ground, with its color smooth and well-proportioned, rich, and elegant. Three peonies are drawn in yellow, pink and white on the coral red glaze ground, the stamens cover the entire picture, the petals are stack-up and blooming, the branches are stretching gracefully, the colors on the vase are varied, and the workmanship is exquisite. The leaves on the vase are well-dotted, and the light and the shade are charming, which switch from green to yellow gradually and naturally. The four Chinese characters in regular script meaning "Made in Tuisi Hall" are inscribed on the white glaze of the bottom.

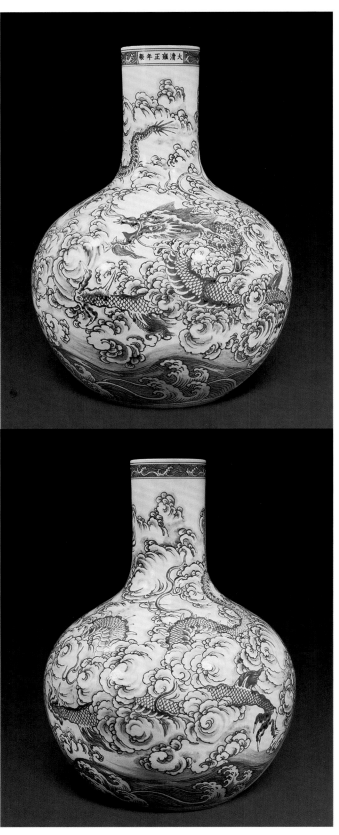

Blue-and-white Underglaze Red Celestial-sphere-shaped Vase with Sea, Cloud and Dragon Patterns

Origin: Reign of Emperor Yongzheng of the Qing Dynasty
Height: 51 cm
Hammer Price: RMB 15,182,400
Name of Auction Company:
Hong Kong Sotheby's
Date of Transaction: 2004-10-31

This porcelain vase has a straight mouth, along neck, a bulged round belly and a round foot. Painted all over are blue-and-white patterns and underglaze red, sea waves are painted near the rim and its belly is mainly painted with sea and dragon patterns. The robust dragon has three claws and a widely opened mouth. There is a line of six characters written in regular script "Made in the Reign of Emperor Yongzheng of the Qing Dynasty" on the rim in blue. With its elegant shape and fine blank, blue-and-white pattern in underglaze red is stable, the paintings and decorations are vivid and exquisite, and it is a fine article of blue-and-white pattern in underglaze red among the official wares during the Reign of Emperor Yongzheng. By that period of time, the workmanship of porcelain making had undergone a dramatic development, reaching the highest level of porcelain making in Chinese history.

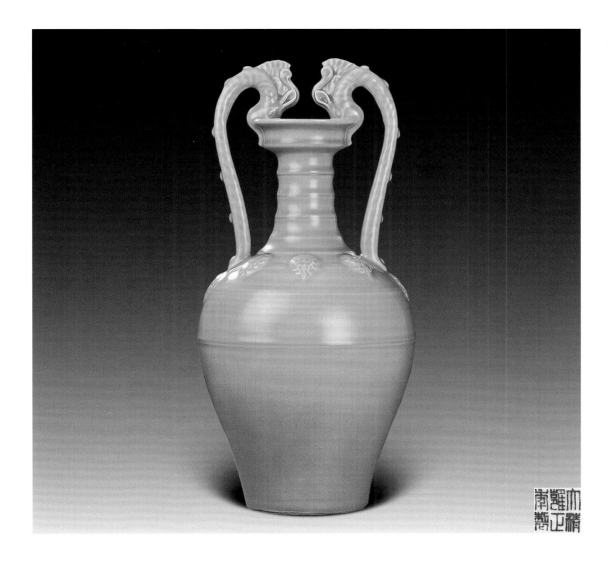

Pea Green Glazed Double-dragon-shaped-eared Vase

Origin: Reign of Emperor Yongzheng of the Qing Dynasty

Height: 51.8 cm

Hammer Price: RMB 18,643,413

Name of Auction Company: Hong Kong Christie's

Date of Transaction: 2004-11-01

This pea green glazed vase has a washer-shaped mouth, a thin neck and a round foot. Painted all over are pea green glaze, and several string patterns are protruding on the surface. Two symmetrical dragon-shaped handles are placed between the shoulders and the mouth with eight elliptical groups of modeling applique. Six seal-script characters in three lines are inscribed on the outside bottom, meaning "Made in the Reign of Emperor Yongzheng of the Qing Dynasty". This is a utensil of regular form and style. With its fine and delicate blank and the bright glaze color, it is truly a precious product made in the imperial kiln in Jingdezhen in imitation of Tang Dynasty white glazed or tri-color double-dragon-shaped-eared vases.

Clashing Color Teapot with Pattern of Playing Kid and Knob

Origin: Reign of Emperor Yongzheng of the Qing Dynasty
Height: 18.9 cm
Hammer Price: RMB 11,751,500
Name of Auction Company: Hong Kong Sotheby's
Date of Transaction: 2007-10-09

This porcelain teapot has a straight mouth, a short neck and a bulged round belly. A circle of curves is painted near the rim. It has an ear-shaped handle and a round lid with a bead-shaped knob. The whole teapot is decorated with a combination of overglaze-color figures and underglaze-color figures. Flowers and plants are painted at the button and the rim is decorated with banana leaf pattern. The pattern of playing kids is painted on the teapot, and six regular-script Chinese characters in two lines meaning "Made in the Reign of Emperor Yongzheng of the Qing Dynasty" are inscribed on the outside bottom in blue-and-white glaze.

Famille Rose Plate with Patterns of Nine Peaches

Origin: Reign of Emperor Yongzheng of the Qing Dynasty
Diameter: 51 cm
Hammer Price: RMB 9,632.000
Name of Auction Company: Beijing Hanhai
Date of Transaction: 2007-06-25

This plate has an outward-sloping mouth, an arc wall and a round foot. The whole famille rose porcelain plate is painted with white-glaze. The peach tree on the bottom is stretching its branches all over the plate. There are nine peaches on the tree, six inside and three outside. Several red bats are flying beside the branches. Six regular-script characters in two lines meaning "Made in the Reign of Emperor Yongzheng of the Qing Dynasty" are inscribed in blue-and-white glaze on the outside bottom. This plate is big in size and elegant in form and structure, and the pattern means "happiness as unbounded as the heaven", and "both happiness and longevity".

Famille Rose Pieced Vase with Gilded Anemone Pattern on Blue Glazed Ground

Origin: Reign of Emperor Qianlong of the Qing Dynasty
Height: 40.6 cm
Hammer Price:
RMB 22,201,435
Name of Auction Company:
Hong Kong Sotheby's
Date of Transaction: 2000-05-02

This vase has a labial mouth, a long neck, and a plump shoulder, a bulged belly and a round foot. Its three parts, the inner bottle, the outside bottle and the base, were fired separately. The inner bottle is connected with the vase in the interior. Unlike other circular revolving vases, this one is a hexagon. Gilded lines are painted alongside the rim and the foot, and blue glaze is the main color of the rim. Auspicious clouds and twining flowers are painted on the bottle in famille rose. Its rim and belly are painted in caramel. Banana leaf pattern is decorated on the rim and the foot. Lotuses are painted on the belly and pierced medallion patterns are carved on the belly as well. Six Chinese characters meaning "Made in the Reign of Emperor Qianlong of the Qing Dynasty" are inscribed on the bottom. Its regular form and style, bright colors, dense grains and delicate craftsmanship make the vase permeated with the combined characteristics of China and the West. The gilded pasqueflower pattern painted on light brown ground represents an impressive "European style" through its color, shade and light and lines. The workmanship of this vase combines famille rose, blue-and-white color as well as piercing art, with a high standard of science and technology. This vase shows the superb workmanship of porcelain making of imperial kilns during the Reign of Emperor Qianlong of the Qing Dynasty.

Vase with Famille Rose Twining Flower Pattern and Concave Brocade Design on Carmine Ground

Origin: Reign of Emperor Qianlong of the Qing Dynasty

Height: 37.5cm

Hammer Price:

RMB 44,407,568

Name of Auction Company:

Hong Kong Sotheby's

Date of Transaction: 2004-10-31

This vase has a slightly outward-sloping mouth, a short neck, a plump and round shoulder, a bulged belly and a round foot. Painted all over is carmine-glaze, different twining flower patterns are drawn after the concave brocade design on carmine ground, and six regular-script characters meaning "Made in the Reign of Emperor Qianlong of the Qing Dynasty" are inscribed on the outside bottom. The arrangement of colors is particularly taken into consideration, and the process of carmine-glazing as the background is unique. This vase is one of the precious representatives of porcelains made in imperial kilns in the Reign of Emperor Qianlong.

 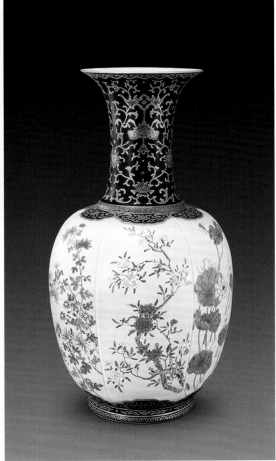

Famille Rose Shiny Blue Gilded Vase with Flower Pattern

Origin: Reign of Emperor Qianlong of the Qing Dynasty

Height: 65 cm

Hammer Price: RMB 24,080,000

Name of Auction Company: Beijing Hanhai

Date of Transaction: 2007-06-25

This vase has an outward-sloping mouth, a thin and long neck, a hexagonal belly and a round foot. The neck and the round foot are gilded with a design in shiny blue. Six groups of flower patterns are painted on the frame of the hexagonal belly. They are peony, cottonrose hibiscus, plum bloosom, chrysanthemum, pomegranate and lotus flowers. Plum bloosom stands for cleanliness and honesty, chrysanthemum means longevity, pomegranate refers to proliferation of offspring, lotus flower symbolize harmonious marriage; peony refers to scholarly honor or official rank and wealth; and cottonrose hibiscus is the symbol of high position and great wealth. Emperor Qianlong cherished a great love for flowers all his life, especially in the first twenty years of his reign. This vase shows the unmatched workmanship of porcelain making in the heyday of the Reign of Emperor Qianlong.

Enamel Painted Wealth and Rank Lantern

Origin: Reign of Emperor Qianlong of the Qing Dynasty
Height: 13.8 cm
Hammer Price: RMB 84,000,000
Name of Auction Company: Sungari International
Date of Transaction: 2007-08-20

   This enamel painted lantern has an inward-sloping mouth, an arc belly and a round foot. The enamel pattern of wealth and rank is painted on the surface of the vessel. There are a towering osmanthus tree and blooming cottonrose hibiscuses. A child is standing under the tree with a bamboo pole. A lady leans against the giant rock in a long dress with a smile on her face, elegant and leisurely. She smells the cottonrose hibiscus in her hand, and there is a basket filled with chrysanthemums and morning glories beside her. A child facing the lady has a ruyi in his hand, turning his head around and looking for something. The maidservant behind him holds in her arms a baby with a rattle-drum. A verse in the running hand is inscribed on the lantern. The four regular-script characters meaning "Made in the Reign of Emperor Qianlong" are inscribed in blue. The bright colors, graceful ladies and lovely kids make the whole picture full of interest and taste.

Blue-and-white Drinking Vessel with Twining Lotus Pattern (made under the supervision of Tang Ying)

Origin: Reign of Emperor Qianlong of the Qing Dynasty
Height: 64.1cm
Hammer Price: RMB 66,080,000
Name of Auction Company: Beijing Council International
Date of Transaction: 2010-12-04

This porcelain vessel has an outward-sloping mouth, a long neck, a bulged belly and a tall round foot. Painted all over is blue-and-white, with twining lotus pattern on the thirteen layers of the vessel. The neatly painted lotus, the auspicious cloud and the twining lotus pattern are typical decorations on blue-and-white porcelain of the Reign of Emperor Qianlong. A brief introduction to Tang Ying, the supervisor, was written on the middle of its body. It has a fine, tough and smooth blank and the overall painting is of average color and slightly blue-and-white. This vessel has a fine gloss, and the blue-and-white glaze is bright. It was painted with the first-class glaze of Zhejiang Province. The exact time of production provides an important clue to the investigation of porcelain development in the Reign of Emperor Qianlong, and the official title serves as a major reference for the understanding of the politics, culture and social life of the time period concerned.

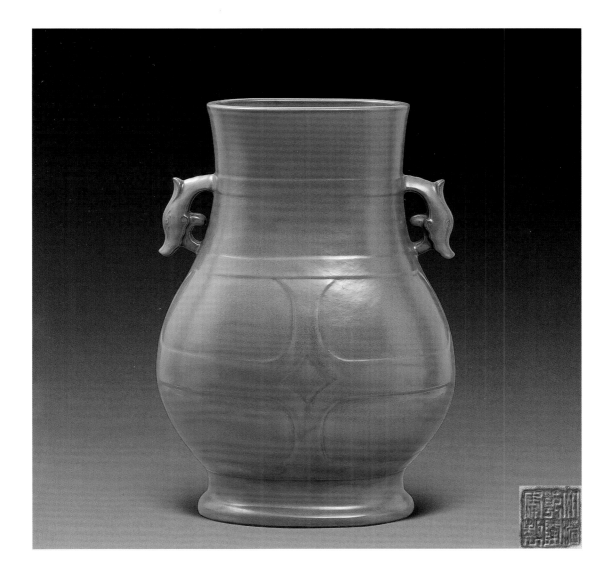

Tea Dust Glazed Pot with Animal-shaped Ears

Origin: Reign of Emperor Qianlong of the Qing Dynasty
Height: 51.5 cm
Hammer Price: RMB 5,712,000
Name of Auction Company: Sungari International
Date of Transaction: 2007-08-20

As an imitation of ancient bronzeware, this pot has an elliptical and slightly outward-sloping mouth, a broad neck, a bulged belly and a round foot. There are a pair of symmetrical ears on two sides of the neck. Painted all over is tea dust glaze and convex grid patterns are decorated on the belly. Six characters in three lines meaning"Made in the Reign of the Emperor Qianlong of the Qing Dynasty"are inscribed on the outside bottom. Delicately and elegantly designed and made, this pot is a typical colored glaze porcelain during the Reign of Emperor Qianlong.

Ruyi Vase with Famille Rose Happiness, Longevity and Hornless Dragon Patterns on Turquoise Green Ground

Origin: Reign of Emperor Jiaqing of the Qing Dynasty

Height: 34.2 cm   Hammer Price: RMB 6,820,000

Name of Auction Company: Beijing Hanhai

Date of Transaction: 2006-12-18

    This vase has a folded rim on which is ruyi-shaped cloud pattern, a contracted neck, a bulged belly and a round foot. There are a pair of symmetrical ruyi-shaped ears on two sides of the neck and wan-shaped ribbons are hanging from the ears. This vase is decorated with turquoise green glaze and famille rose, the cloud pattern is painted along the rim, and lotus patterns are painted on the belly, mixed with hornless dragons, bats, halberds and peaches. Lotus and fretwork patterns are decorated around the shin and the foot. Six seal-script characters in three lines meaning"Made in the Reign of Emperor Jiaqing of the Qing Dynasty"are inscribed on the outside bottom in red glaze.

Eight Treasures on Famille Rose Lotus Receptacles

Origin: Reign of Emperor Jiaqing of the Qing Dynasty

Height: 24 cm   Hammer Price: RMB 4,256,000

Name of Auction Company: Sungari International

Date of Transaction: 2007-08-20

There are eight treasures on famille rose lotus receptacles, with the bases shaped like inverted plates, the columns in the shape of flowers and leaves, and lotus seedpods at the top. Eight pierced circular auspicious things, Dharma-cakra, Conch, Umbrella, Baigai, Lotus, Holy Jar, Goldfish and Panzhang are placed on the receptacles. They are all in famille rose glaze and gilded. The bottoms of these receptacles are decorated with turquoise green glaze. In the blank of the bottom, six seal-script characters in three lines meaning "Made in the Reign of Emperor Jiaqing of the Qing Dynasty" are inscribed in alum-red glaze. They were used for worshipping the Buddha. These exquisitely-made and well-preserved articles are rare treasures in famille rose porcelain of the Reign of Emperor Jiaqing.

Blue-and-white Famille Rose Square Vase with Pattern of the Eighteen Arhats

Origin: Reign of Emperor Daoguang of the Qing Dynasty
Height: 30.5 cm
Hammer Price: RMB 330,000
Name of Auction Company: Beijing Hanhai
Date of Transaction: 1997-06-01

This square vase has an outward-sloping mouth, a broad neck, square and bended shoulders, a slightly concave belly and a round foot. On each side of the bottle are gilded lines, blue-and-white famille rose are painted all over the vase, twining lotuses are painted in blue-and-white on the neck, and Eighteen Arhats are painted in famille rose on its belly. A symmetrical pair of dragons is painted on the foot. Four regular-script characters meaning "Made in Shende Hall" are inscribed on the outside bottom. With its bright color and magnificent design, it is truly a fine article among imperial kiln porcelain of the Reign of Emperor Daoguang of the Qing Dynasty.

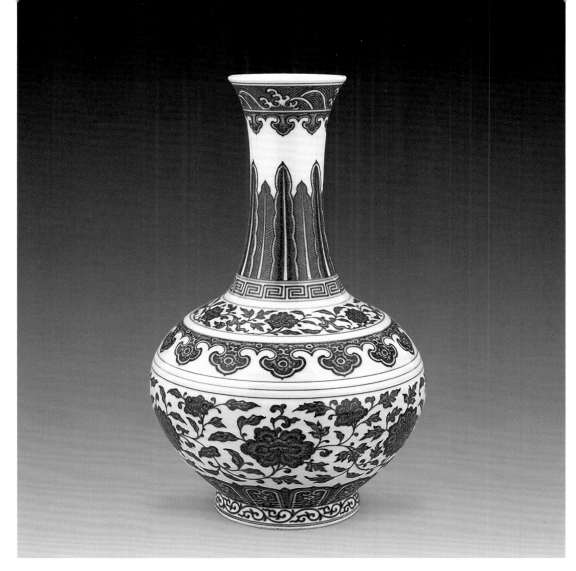

Blue-and-white Vase with Twining Lotus Pattern

Origin: Reign of Emperor Xianfeng of the Qing Dynasty
Height: 38 cm
Hammer Price: RMB 880,000
Name of Auction Company: Liaoning International
Date of Transaction: 2005-09-27

This vase has an outward-sloping mouth, a long and contracted neck, a flat and round belly and a round foot. Painted all over are blue-and-white glaze. The rim is painted with sea and cloud patterns, banana leaf and fret patterns are painted on the neck, lotus and cloud patterns are painted on the shoulders, twining lotus patterns are painted on the shin, lotus petal pattern is painted near the foot, and curved grass patterns are decorated on the foot. Six regular-script characters in two lines meaning "Made in the Reign of Emperor Xianfeng of the Qing Dynasty"are inscribed in blue-and-white on the outside bottom. All the patterns are elegant and in good order, the composition of the picture is well-arranged and the blue-and-white glaze is verdant. All these features make this article a rare treasure of imperial kiln porcelain in the Reign of Emperor Xianfeng.

Blue-and-white Case with Flower Pattern

Origin: Reign of Emperor Tongzhi of the Qing Dynasty

Diameter: 26 cm

Hammer Price:
RMB 528,000

Name of Auction Company:
China Guardian

Date of Transaction:
2005-05-15

This porcelain case is in the shape of a steamed bun with a round foot, with the upper and the lower mouths combined together. The interior is painted with white glaze and the exterior is painted with bended branch patterns. T-shaped blue-and-white patterns are painted on the rims of the upper and lower mouths and on the outside wall of its round foot. Four seal-script characters in blue-and-white meaning "Made in the Tihe Palace" are inscribed on the outside bottom. The porcelain case is beautifully shaped and neatly painted and inscribed.

Light Crimson Square Vase with Animal-shaped Ears and Calligraphy and Paintings by Cheng Men and Jin Pinqing

Origin: Reign of Emperor Tongzhi of the Qing Dynasty

Height: 57 cm   Height: 56 cm

Hammer Price: RMB 666,000

Name of Auction Company: Beijing Chieftown

Date of Transaction: 2010-06-21

These two square vases have outward-sloping mouths, bended shoulders, bulged bellies and round feet. On each side of the shoulder is an animal-shaped ear. The whole body is painted with landscapes and figures with colored decorations in white glaze and light crimson. These two vases are sizable in shape and exquisite in workmanship. The refreshing design of painting and natural and unrestrained artistic style make these two a poetic beauty and a perfect pair. The Chinese lunar year inscribed on these two vases is a rare material of great historical value in the study of the life time and artistic style of Cheng Men and Jin Pinqing.

Black Colored Basin on Yellow Ground with Lotus and Egret Patterns

Origin: Reign of Emperor Guangxu of the Qing Dynasty
Diameter: 32 cm
Hammer Price: RMB 101,200
Name of Auction Company: Beijing Hanhai
Date of Transaction: 2001-12-10

This basin has a folded rim, a straight wall and a round foot. The whole body is black colored on yellow ground. Bat and cloud patterns are painted around the rim and bended flowers are painted on the inner and outer walls. The inside bottom of the basin is painted with egrets, lotuses and reeds as the main decorative patterns, which mean"Passing imperial exams at all levels in a row". The outer bottom bears the four-seal-script-character inscription in red color meaning "Made in Tihe Palace".

Famille Rose Bowl with Flower and Bird Patterns on Green Ground

Origin: Reign of Emperor Guangxu of the Qing Dynasty

Diameter: 10.5 cm

Hammer Price: RMB 82,500

Name of Auction Company: Beijing Hanhai

Date of Transaction: 1997-12-20

This bowl has an open mouth, an arc belly and a round foot. The whole body is decorated with famille rose on green ground, and the rim is painted with thin gilded lines. Inside the bowl are grape patterns and outside the bowl are flower patterns. The exquisite quality and superb workmanship make this bowl a fine item of porcelain produced by imperial kilns in the Reign of Emperor Guangxu.

Famille Rose Jar with Magpie and Plum Patterns

Origin: Reign of Emperor Guangxu of the Qing Dynasty

Diameter: 48 cm

Hammer Price: RMB 168,000

Name of Auction Company: China Guardian

Date of Transaction: 2009-03-28

This jar has a folded rim, an arc belly and a round foot. It is decorated all over with white glaze famille rose, and the rim is painted with four sets of flower and plant patterns. Inside the jar are swimming fish patterns and outside the jar are magpies on plum trees meaning "Happy expressions appear on the eyebrows", which symbolizes the comings of good luck, happiness and fortune.

Famille Rose Plate with Pattern of Promising Kid

Origin: Reign of Emperor Xuantong of the Qing Dynasty
Diameter: 23.1 cm
Hammer Price: RMB 88,000
Name of Auction Company: Beijing Hanhai
Date of Transaction: 2001-07-02

This plate has an open mouth, a shallow arc wall and a round foot. The inside wall is decorated with famille rose on yellow ground with decorative patterns of various types of twining flowers, and in the center are bended flower patterns. The outside wall is decorated with famille rose on white ground with three sets of decorative flower patterns. At the bottom is an inscription indicating that this plate was produced in the Reign of Emperor Xuantong of the Qing Dynasty.

Underglaze Famille Rose Vase with Flower and Bird Patterns

Origin: Reign of Emperor Xuantong of the Qing Dynasty

Height: 52 cm   Hammer Price: RMB 649,600

Name of Auction Company: Beijing Poly

Date of Transaction: 2010-10-23

This vase has an outward-sloping mouth, a contracted neck, a bulged belly and a round foot. The whole article is decorated with underglaze five-color decorationson white ground, and the rim is painted with patterns of twining flowers. On its belly are decorative patterns of flowers and birds. This porcelain vase has a graceful design with a simple but elegant style, expressing the wishes for wealth, rank and auspiciousness.

Dehua Kiln White Porcelain Statue of Goddess of Mercy (Avalokitesvara)

Origin: Qing Dynasty
Height: 83.2 cm
Hammer Price: RMB 430,675
Name of Auction Company: Hong Kong Christie's
Date of Transaction:1999-11-02

This statue of the Goddess of Mercy wears a high crown with pearl and jade necklaces ornamented on the chest. Its facial countenance is abundant with a serene facial expression. It stands on a lotus receptacle, wearing a wide-sleeved kasaya. This porcelain is ivory white and has a smooth glazed surface like other fine porcelain produced in Dehua Kiln of the Ming and Qing Dynasties, such as the white glazed statue of Bodhidharma and other white glazed porcelain statues.

VIII. Pottery and Porcelain of the Republic of China

Famille Rose Vase with Figures in a Frame

Origin: Republic of China

Dimension: 20 cm×12 cm

Hammer Price: RMB 3,740,000

Name of Auction Company: Shanghai Jinghua

Date of Transaction: 2007-12-21

This vase has an outward-sloping mouth, a contracted neck, a deep belly and a round foot. Its composition arrangement is imitated from imperial kiln porcelain made during the Reign of Emperor Qianlong. All its body is painted with chrysanthemum petals with famille rose in an exquisite style, and the frame is decorated with a picture of young imperial ladies. Four regular-script Chinese characters meaning "Made in the Reign of Emperor Qianlong" is inscribed in iron red. The impressive and superb workmanship makes it a masterpiece of porcelain made by Shi Dezhi in the period of the Republic of China in imitation of famille rose porcelain produced in imperial kilns in the Reign of Emperor Qianlong.

Famille Rose Double-dragon-shaped-eared Vase with Wealth and Rank Patterns

Origin: Republic of China

Height: 30.1 cm   Hammer Price: RMB 418,000

Name of Auction Company: Beijing Hanhai

Date of Transaction: 2005-06-20

This vase has a plate-shaped mouth, a long neck, plump shoulders, a sloping belly, two dragon-shaped ears and a double-ring foot. At the bottom of the foot is an inscription in two frames decorated with red color and gold paintings. Near the gilded rim are patterns of fretwork with blue color. Under its rim are ruyi patterns and its ears are decorated with gold paintings and red color. The whole body is decorated with patterns of peonies, bamboos and gilded phoenixes and the foot is decorated with shou (longevity) patterns. Judging from the six blooming peonies, this was meant to be a present for Cao Kun's sixtieth birthday. The regular design, pure-white blank, smooth glaze and elaborative patterns make this article a fine imitation of porcelain of the Sui and Tang Dynasties.

Hongxian-styled Famille Rose Gilded Vase with Patterns of Playing Kids (one pair)

Origin: Republic of China
Height: 12 cm
Hammer Price: RMB 165,000
Name of Auction Company: Liaoning Zone
Date of Transaction: 2007-06-10

This vase has a round plate-shaped mouth, a contracted neck with a convex string pattern, plump shoulders, a bulged belly and a round foot. The entire body is decorated with famille rose in white glaze, and the rim, the neck and the foot are painted with patterns of fretwork, clouds, lotus petals and banana leaves. Around the belly are bamboo forest, rocks, and lawns with 16 children playing on the lawn and behind the rocks. At the bottom is an inscription indicating the year of production. The lifelike figures and the riot of the colors of famille rose make this vase a delicate and exquisite treasure.

Blue-and-white Five-color Vase with Scenes from "A Dream of the Red Mansion"

Origin: Republic of China
Diameter of Belly: 28 cm
Height: 73 cm
Hammer Price: RMB 286,000
Name of Auction Company: Shanghai Jiatai
Date of Transaction: 2004-11-30

This vase has an outward-sloping mouth, a contracted neck, a round shoulder, an arc belly and a round foot. The vase is in full glaze and the blank is exposed on the ridge of the foot. The fine and compact body, neat design and white glaze as lustrous and smooth as jade, together with its even glazing make it a rare treasure. Around the body is a blue-and-white five-colored scene from "A Dream of the Red Mansion" depicting as many as thirty women visiting a park with pavilions, courtyards, phoenix trees, bamboos and stones.

Carmine Medallion Vase with Landscape and Figure Paintings

Origin: Republic of China
Height: 28.5 cm
Hammer Price: RMB 242,000
Name of Auction Company: Shanghai Jinghua
Date of Transaction: 2005-12-22

This vase has an outward-sloping mouth, a contracted neck, a bulged belly and a round foot. The entire body is decorated with famille rose on carmine ground. Painted inside the medallion on the belly are landscapes and figures. This is a rare precious porcelain in the period of the Republic of China.

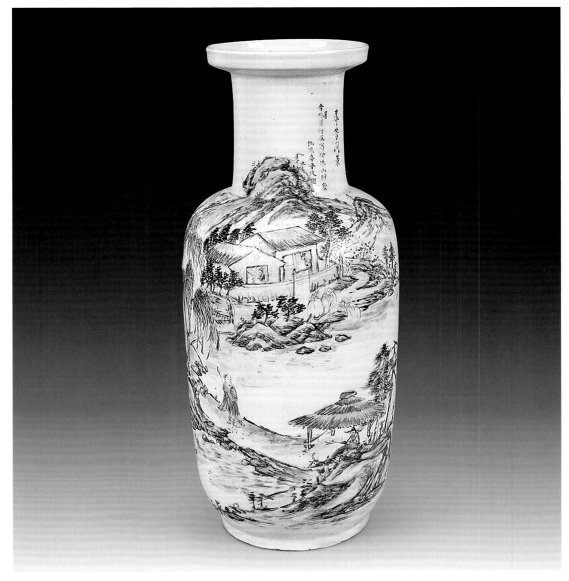

Light Crimson Vase with Landscape and Figure Paintings

Origin: Republic of China

Height: 45 cm

Hammer Price: RMB 143,000

Name of Auction Company: Nanjing Shizhuzhai

Date of Transaction: 2005-12-16

This vase has a plate-shaped mouth, a straight neck and a cylindrical belly. It is shaped like a spindle, hence the name"spindle-shaped vase". The whole body is painted with landscapes and figures in light crimson. The inscription on the neck indicates the time, place and context of the composition of the poem and the author of the poem. There is also a seal-script inscription meaning"Made in the Reign of Emperor Xuande of the Qing Dynasty". The composition is delicate and the painting is elaborative.

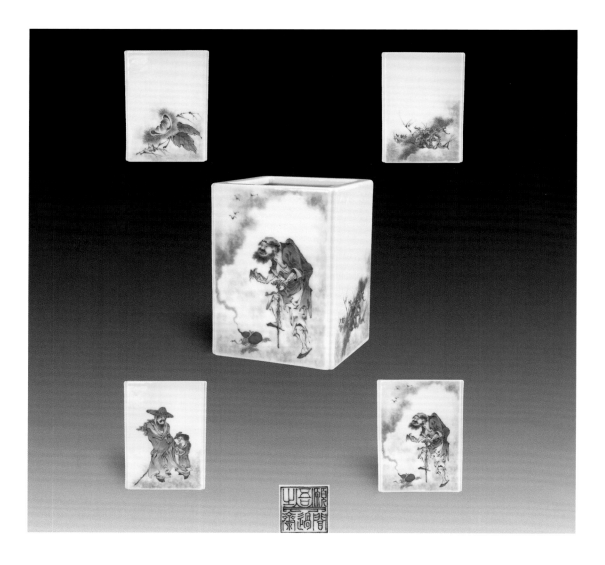

Blue-and-white Square Brush Holder with Figure Paintings by Wang Bu

Origin: Republic of China
Height: 16.2 cm
Hammer Price: RMB 3,355,000
Name of Auction Company: Tianjin Cultural Relics
Date of Transaction: 2007-12-11

This square brush holder has straight walls and a round foot, with decorative patterns on four sides. One side is painted with an old man with big eyes and a shaggy beard. He wears a headband and carries a bamboo hat on his back. He has a walking stick in one hand and a bat in the other. Blue smoke is coming out of the calabash on the ground, as if he is in a fairyland. The other three sides are painted with a hermit and a lad, pine trees and ganoderma, respectively. The smooth and exquisite lines of the figures and sturdy branches of the pine tree show the superb painting skills of Wang Bu. There is an inscription at the bottom.

Famille Rose Porcelain Plates with Landscape Paintings (a set of four plates)

Origin: Republic of China
Height: 72 cm
Width: 8.5 cm
Hammer Price: RMB 2,750,000
Name of Auction Company: Shanghai Xinren
Date of Transaction: 2005-12-04

This set of four rectangular plates is decorated with landscape paintings in famille rose. The paintings are masterpieces of Wang Yeting in 1926, or the 15th year of the Republic of China. The colors are fresh but not gaudy, and well-matched but not thick. The neat and intricate painting style and the well-arranged composition present the beauty of the four seasons. The paintings are both delicate and grand, and the scenes are both tranquil and far-reaching.

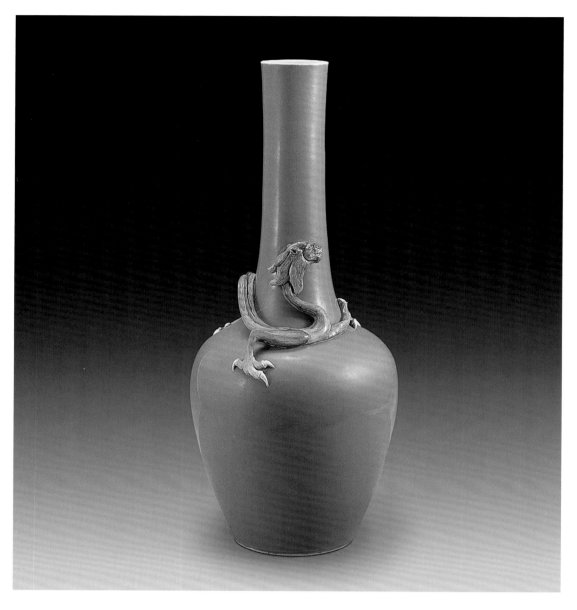

Blue Glazed Carmine Vase with Hornless Dragon Pattern

Origin: Republic of China

Height: 50.5 cm   Hammer Price: RMB 165,000

Name of Auction Company: Beijing Hanhai

Date of Transaction: 2001-07-02

This vase has a slightly outward-sloping mouth, a long and thin neck, a bulged belly and a round foot. It is decorated all over with blue glaze and has patterns except for a three-claw dragon on carmine ground. The regular form, fine blank, smooth glaze and original color make the vase a fine artwork during the Republic of China. It bears a seal-script inscription meaning "Made in the 1st Year of Jiangxi Porcelain Industrial Corporation".

Famille Rose Plate with Flower and Branch Pattern

Origin: Republic of China

Diameter: 41 cm

Hammer Price: RMB 121,000

Name of Auction Company: Beijing Tranthy

Date of Transaction: 2003-09-21

This plate has an open mouth, an arc belly and a round foot. It is decorated all over with white glaze famille rose. Branch and flower patterns cover the whole plate. There is a seal-shaped inscription at the bottom of the plate.

Enamel Colored Bowl with Painting "Inquiring about the Ferry at Taoyuan" by Liu Linggu (made under the supervision of Liang Duishi)

Origin: Republic of China

Diameter: 12.8 cm

Hammer Price: RMB 407,000

Name of Auction Company: Beijing ChengXuan

Date of Transaction: 2006-11-24

This enamel colored bowl has a slightly outward-sloping rim, an arc belly and a round foot. The extremely light and thin blank is the characteristic of a new variety in the Republic of China. It is decorated all over with enamel color. The rim is painted with ruyi patterns in red and blue, the center is painted with dragons and flowers, and the outer wall is painted with the scene of a famous story entitled "Inquiring about the Ferry at Taoyuan", which has the implication of the pursuit of knowledge and skill. The aflutter willows and lifelike figures are painted with superb workmanship. The inscription and many well-known figures in the Republic of China who were related to this bowl make it a rare treasure in Chinese porcelain.